GROPINGS AFTER TRUTH:

A LIFE JOURNEY

FROM

NEW ENGLAND CONGREGATIONALISM

TO THE

One Catholic and Apostolic Church.

BY

JOSHUA HUNTINGTON

NEW YORK:
THE CATHOLIC PUBLICATION SOCIETY,
No. 9 BARCLAY STREET.

PREFACE.

THE author of the book herewith presented to the reading community has requested me to stand as sponsor to his first literary offspring. I have undertaken this office with pleasure, on account both of the intrinsic value and merit of the volume, and also of the special interest and familiarity of the topics contained in its pages. It describes the interior history of a mind travelling from Puritanism to the Catholic Church over a long and circuitous route. The writer who thus describes the process of his own conversion is a genuine son of New England, descended from ancestors who, from the first settlement of the colonies, have been honorably distinguished in church and state, educated from infancy in the pure tradition of the pilgrim fathers, a pupil of the ablest teachers of Yale, Princeton, and Andover sincere and earnest in his disposition, and therefore a competent witness regarding those things of which he speaks. The history of such a mind is not purely individual, but also representative; the mental analysis of a very perfect specimen of a large class, completely disappointed by New England theology, and yearning for a doctrine more satisfactory to the demands of reason, the dictates of conscience, and the wants of the soul. It refutes the allegation that the tendency toward the Catholic Church is confined to the small section of High-Church Episcopalians. This allegation has an appearance of truth from the fact that several converts to the Catholic Church from the unhierarchical denominations have passed through the middle region of Anglicanism. The author of this book also tarried awhile at the half-way house. This only proves, however, that prejudice against the Roman Church, ignorance of the true state of the question, and hereditary prepossession in favor of everything English have deluded their imagination for a time. The movement toward the Episcopal Church, which was initiated by Dr. Cutler, a former president of Yale College, itself proves a tendency toward Catholicity; although in a majority of instances the individuals who have felt it have stopped short of the logical and legitimate result of the church principles they have adopted. From various causes, so well known that I need not specify them, our English and American books of controversy have been chiefly occupied with refuting the illusory claim of the Episcopal Church to a catholic character, and proving that church principles logically require submission to the supreme authority of Rome. The present volume takes another course, and traces the course of thought leading from popular Protestantism to the Catholic Church. It must prove, consequently, very interesting and useful to a large class of persons whose case is not adequately handled by the writers above alluded to.

The popular Protestant theology has two fatal defects: The first is. that it furnishes no certain or exact criterion of doctrine; the second, that it gives no sufficient rule of action. It cannot tell a man what he must believe or what he must do in order to be a true follower of Christ and child of God. Its failure has become so manifest as to produce a very general suspicion that perhaps there is no positive religion revealed by God, but that, if there be one, it is the religion taught by the Catholic Church. There is, therefore, a twofold tendency, on one side to scepticism, on the other hand to a return to the bosom of Catholic unity. The first is the beginning of a suicidal mania; the second, an impulse toward a new and more vigorous life. This impulse will be quickened and directed in many souls, I doubt not, by the present volume; and it is my heartfelt wish that every one who reads it may attain to the same faith and peace in the true fold of Christ, in which the struggles, doubts, and anxious inquiries of the author have so happily terminated. AUGUSTINE F. HEWIT.

ST. PAUL'S, NEW YORK, Feast of the Assumption, 1868.

GROPINGS AFTER TRUTH.

MY DEAR ——:

I have decided upon a step which will probably strike you with astonishment and dismay, but to which I am impelled by an imperative sense of duty. I have become a Catholic, or, as you and I have always expressed it, a Romanist. I have accepted, as true and divine, doctrines which I often joined with you in ridiculing; I have become addicted to practices which we have agreed in regarding as superstitious and idolatrous. But I assure you that this is no sudden freak of mine. Though you have been entirely unaware of it, my views in regard to the Catholic Church have been undergoing a process of change for a year and a half; and during the last six months a consideration of my own duty in relation to it has so urged itself upon my mind, that I could not shut it out even had I dared to do so, and this I did not dare even to attempt. Wherever I might be, or in whatever I might be engaged, I would find my thoughts irresistibly drawn back to this one subject, and the more I though f it, the more I became involved in doubt perplexity. Objections to the Catholic faith which had always seemed to be conclusive, would suddenly be swept away by answers presented to my mind with such force and distinctness that they appeared to be spoken in my ears; and I could not in some cases resist the conviction that these thoughts, so new to me then, though I have since read them in Catholic books, were not my own, but were suggested by some intelligence exterior to myself. I became convinced that it was possible, at all events, that it was the "still, small voice" of the Spirit of God which was compelling me to listen; and so long as there existed the smallest possibility of this, I did not dare to stop my ears. It was while I was in this state of mind that S——, who had become somewhat alarmed at a remark made by me in a letter to M——, wrote me that she wished I would not let myself be drawn into taking too much interest in the Catholic religion. The caution was well-meant, but it came too late. It is all well enough to advise a man to shut his eyes and walk boldly forward, so long as he is quite sure the way before him is straight and level; but let his suspicions be aroused in the slightest degree that his path ends in a precipice, and he will prefer to see where he is going.

I wish you to be convinced, also, that I have not depended upon my own wisdom in searching for a solution of my perplexities. I have been deeply impressed throughout with a sense of my weakness and ignorance, and of my utter dependence upon the guidance of Almighty God; and my prayer to him and to our blessed Lord has been constant and unceasing, night and day, that he would teach me his will. I have cried to him as did the blind beggar of Jericho: "Jesus, Son of David, have mercy on me: Lord, that I may receive my sight!" Do you think he has turned away from my despairing supplication? that he has left me to wander into errors and deceits that will offend him and lead me to destruction? If you can think so, I cannot; I know in whom I have trusted, and I know that his arm is under me, and that, resting on it, I cannot fall.

And now I am going to give you a detailed account of the religious experiences through which I have passed, in order that you may understand how I have come at last into my present position. Though you may have known me all my life, yet you know me only externally. You know that I became a professing Christian when in college; that three years afterward I renounced my faith in Christ and fell into infidelity; that ten years later I suddenly, as it seemed to you, abandoned my scepticism and renewed my connection with the church, and that since, for a period of nearly twenty years, I have appeared to be at rest in my religious faith. But you will learn, no doubt to your surprise, as I have never been in the habit of talking about myself, that I have been wandering in a fog all my life; that my religious opinions have been undergoing one change after another, year after year, and that never, until I was led by God's grace into the Catholic Church, have I felt sure that I was not standing upon a treacherous sand-bank, that would be washed away and leave me to be swallowed up in the flood.

I hope you will read my narrative with the kindness and affection which you have always manifested for me, and that, having read it, you will accuse me of nothing worse than folly and stupidity. As I can conceive of no possible advantage in a worldly point of view which I can derive from becoming a Catholic, I am sure you will at least give me credit for sincerity, and I hope you will admit there is some show of sense even in my foolishness.

Until within a year and a half ago, I had never had a suspicion that the views might be false in which we had been educated with regard to the Church of Rome. We had been taught to consider that church as the Antichrist which was to come in the latter days; as the embodiment of wickedness in its vilest form; wickedness concealing itself in the external garb of purity. When a boy, I should have been struck with the most incredulous amazement had I heard the idea suggested, (which I certainly never did,) that a Roman Catholic might possibly be a good man and a sincere Christian; and my only idea of the Pope was that derived from Bunyan's representation of him, as sitting at the mouth of his den, like a disabled wild beast, vainly gnashing his teeth at the pilgrims on their way to the Eternal City. "Pope and Pagan" were always associated in my mind as twin monsters, equally enemies of God and man.

When, as I became older, I found that there had been good men in the Catholic Church, I was astonished, but I accepted the explanation offered, that they were exceptional cases—good in spite of their religion, just as Plato was a good man in spite of his paganism.

When J—— became a convert to the Catholic religion, I was amazed at his infatuation, and unable to understand how a man, who seemed to possess good sense in other things, should betray such an utter want of it in this; and I confidently anticipated that he would soon discover the emptiness of his new faith, and would abandon it as he had abandoned other opinions which at various times he had adopted. But when I found that his faith in his church grew stronger from year to year, and that his confidence in the piety of her clergy increased as his acquaintance with them was extended, I was compelled to modify my own opinions. I had no doubt of the piety and purity of purpose of both J—— and M——, and it was incredible that they could be deceived for so many years in regard to the true character of the large circle of Catholics, many of whom were clergymen, with whom they were constantly associating. I came gradually, therefore, to the conclusion that my old idea, that "Romanism" is not Christianity at all, but only a sort of modified paganism, must be erroneous, and that the Roman Church holds, at bottom, the essential doctrines of the Christian religion, though almost smothered under corruptions of human invention; but I never suspected for a moment that the peculiar doctrines of that church which are condemned by Protestant sects, are anything else than corruptions, nor that there is any foundation for the claim which she makes to be the "One Holy Catholic Apostolic Church," the spouse of Christ. It was with perfect sincerity that I more than once declared, that I considered myself under no more obligation to investigate her claims to my faith and obedience, than those of Hindooism or Mohammedanism.

And now go back with me to the days of our childhood, and let us together retrace the interior spiritual life through which I have been led for half a century, and of which you have known nothing. You remember the kind of religious teaching and influence under which, as children we were brought up. I knew nothing about it except that I heard every one call it "Calvinism;" and I supposed Calvinism and Christianity to be merely different names of the same thing, and that a denial of the doctrines of Calvin and of Christ involved equal guilt, and would equally result in eternal damnation. I do not mean to say that I was ever taught this in so many words; it was, however, the product in my own mind of the teachings which I received. The result in the mind of a child of the religious instruction which is given him would often amaze the teacher if he were able to discover it. He pours in his doctrines as a chemist would pour acids into what he regards as an empty flask, expecting them to remain unchanged at the bottom. But the flask is not empty; it contains unsuspected earths and alkalies, and the resulting compound is something very different from the liquid which was poured in. I, of course, derived all my ideas in regard to religion from our mother, and other relatives who held the same opinions as herself, and I implicitly believed all which they told me; but I believed it as I understood it, and some of the articles of my faith would have astonished them not a little could they have known them. One false idea which I adopted in childhood, and which brought forth its fruit in subsequent years, was, that a true Christian is perfectly free from sin. I can account for this only by supposing that our mother, in taking pains to impress upon my mind a sense of the goodness which results from piety, led me, without being herself aware of it, to infer that a truly pious person is absolutely sinless.

All the feelings which I had in my childhood in connection with religion were disagreeable; I saw it only in a repulsive form. Whatever was pleasant in my daily life was wholly dissociated from all religious bearings or influences; whenever religion came forward, it was always with a stern, repulsive face, to do something which I disliked. It interfered with my sports, checked all my gayety, took away my playthings and picture-books, made me sit still and learn verses and hymns as a task, forbidding me to do what would have given me pleasure, and compelling me to do what I hated. Sunday especially was a dismal day, and I would gladly have blotted it out of the calendar. The only thing that served to relieve its cold and silent monotony was, that twice a day I could exchange the prison atmosphere of home for the privilege of sitting a couple of hours in a high-backed pew, where I could see nothing except the people in the opposite gallery, while sundry elocutionary exercises were performed in the pulpit over my head, to which I paid not the slightest attention, and of which I should have understood nothing, however attentive I might have been. The general result of my early religious training was, a conviction that religion was a very disagreeable thing *to me*, while at the same time I believed that, in some manner mysterious to me, pious people enjoyed it, because they often said it was the source of all their happiness. My inference was, that I found it repulsive because I was not a Christian, but that when I should be converted—a change which I was then much too young to expect for many a year—I should like it as they did. Indeed, there is little doubt that I was told so.

At the age of ten years, and while a school-boy

at Andover Academy, I passed through one of those periods of religious awakening upon which New England Calvinists chiefly depend for the conversion of sinners, and which are known by the technical name of "revivals." Hoping that the time had come when I should be changed from the state of nature in which I had thus far lived, and in which I was liable at any moment to die, to the state of grace in which I should be able to please God, and into which I never doubted the Holy Spirit would sooner or later bring me, I began to pray and read the Bible and attend prayer-meetings, and perform the other acts which are prescribed in such cases, waiting from day to day for some evidence that God had given me a new heart. But my assiduous use of these "means of grace" resulted in nothing, and after a few weeks my excitement wore away as the "revival" died out, and I gave up the attempt to get religion at that time. In the opinion of my kind friends, I had, by my obstinate persistence in sin, "grieved away the Holy Spirit," perhaps "sinned away my day of grace," and there was only too much reason to fear that God would never give me another such call, but would henceforth leave me to work out my own perdition. But these alarming prognostications did not alarm me in the least; for I was perfectly conscious that I had been really anxious to be converted, and had done everything that I knew how to do in order to bring it about. I will explain more fully what I mean by this in the account of my next "awakening."

Four years now passed over, during which, so far as I can now remember, it was never hinted to me that I was required to love and serve God. If any such duty was ever urged upon me, it made no impression upon my mind; for my idea was that I must be converted before there was any use in trying to please God, and that there was no hope of conversion until another revival should overtake me. It was evident to my mind, from the conduct and conversation of the pious persons with whom I was in any manner associated, that these were the opinions held by them. Conversions, except during these periods of religious excitement, were always spoken of as little less than miraculous, and except at these times it was never customary to urge upon the unconverted the duty of becoming Christians. So far as my own experience goes, I can state explicitly that from the time of our mother's death, which occurred when I was eleven years old, though I was constantly living in the families of professing Christians, members of the church, I never received such instruction or warning from any of them as led me really to believe that I ought to become a Christian then, at once. It is possible I may at times have been told so, though even this is very doubtful; for everything in their treatment of me showed, as I have said, that my conversion, during a time of religious quietude, would have been viewed by them with as much astonishment as would a rainbow in a cloudless sky. During this period, if I refrained from vicious practices, lived a moral life, and went to church on Sunday, it appeared to me that I did all which was required or expected of me. My pious friends would probably have been shocked had they known I had such notions, and would say they had never taught them to me. My reply would be, "You certainly never meant to teach me such things, but 'actions speak louder than words,' and I believe you acted in accordance with your opinions."

The next revival through which I passed occurred when I was fourteen years old, and at the Academy at Amherst, Massachusetts. I have a distinct recollection of my mental exercises during that period. I was very anxious to become a Christian, and used to read the Bible and other good books, and pray most unceasingly, and attend prayer-meetings and converse on religious subjects, hoping, hour after hour, and day after day that God would be satisfied with my prayers and tears, and would give me the new heart for which I was begging; but all in vain. The teacher of the school, at whose house I was living, would ask me from time to time whether I "felt any change;" but the only change of which I was conscious was a sense of depression and weariness, and that was, of course, no evidence of conversion. This miserable state of things continued for so long a time that at last, I believe, he became tired of it, and told me that, as I seemed resolved not to yield to the influences of the Holy Spirit, I had better resume my studies, which had been laid aside in order that I might give up my whole time to the more important work of getting religion. So I had sinned through another blessed season of revival, and my prospect of being ever again visited by the Holy Spirit, whose gracious influences I had twice successfully resisted, was very dark indeed.

Now, what did I, and what did my pious advisers, suppose was to happen in the case of my conversion? Simply this: that while I should be engaged in prayer or in holy meditations, I should suddenly be impressed with an overwhelming sense of the goodness of God or of my own wickedness, or both, and should then experience some strange ecstatic feeling, different from anything ever felt before, from which I might derive a vivid assurance that my sins were pardoned, that God had created a new heart within me, and that I was "born again." This was, and is, the New England method of conversion; and the piety of the Christian who has not experienced these supernatural emotions, and who cannot state the precise day and hour when the change took place, is regarded as of very questionable quality.

Persons "under conviction," as the phrase is, are directed to pray, to read the Bible and religious books, to fix their thoughts upon God and holy things, to attend prayer-meetings, and converse with pious people on the subject of the salvation of their souls. These instructions are intelligible and practical, and all these things I did most persistently, something else was evidently requisite, for doing them did not make me a Christian. But when I anxiously asked what more was required, I was answered with the usual cant phrases, that I must "give my heart to God," "yield to the influences of the Holy Spirit," "submit myself to the divine will," and other such expressions, all of which are mere figures of speech which presented no practical idea to my mind. If Almighty God, or one of his angels, had come to me visibly and asked for my heart, I would gladly have given it, provided any way could be contrived of getting it out of my body; or if the divine Spirit had appeared to me and required any external act of submission, I would have complied most joyfully. This plainly was not what my religious teachers expected me to do; but what they did expect, or how I was to do it, I did not know, and they knew just as little. That what was required of me was merely that I should resolve henceforth to endeavor to do the will of God in all things, to strive after holiness, and to avoid all that is sinful—that this was the instruction which I needed, no one ever dreamed; for their theology taught them that such resolutions must come after conversion; that the unconverted man *cannot* make them with sincerity, and that conversion is wholly and only a free gift of God, with which the sinner has nothing to do further than to make some preliminary preparation for it in "using the means of grace." The more assiduously he does this, the more hopeful his case becomes; but having used these means to the best of his ability, his own power ceases, and he can only wait and wonder why he "feels no change."

It is scarcely necessary for me to say, that my conscience did not reproach me in the least degree during the time of my "awakening," for what was represented as my obstinate resistance to the influences of the Holy Spirit. I was often told that God was ready and desirous to save me, and only my own unwillingness was the obstacle in the way. I did not dispute this, but I knew it was not true in any sense intelligible to me. So the solemn declarations of my religious friends, after the excitement was over, that my case was a very alarming one; that God had been striving with me for weeks, endeavoring to overcome my wicked opposition, and had now left me to pursue my chosen way to everlasting death, fell upon my ears as words that might contain some metaphysical truth beyond my comprehension, but which, in their plain, obvious meaning, I was conscious were not true. I had been anxious to become a Christian; I had done everything which I knew how to do to fit myself for the change which could be wrought only by the power of God; and as he had not seen fit to give me a new heart, I admitted that there must have been some deficiency in my own conduct. But being totally ignorant of what that deficiency was, and being conscious that I should have remedied it if it had been explained to me intelligibly, I had no sense of ill-desert in connection with the failure of my attempts to become a Christian. I was told that it was my duty to give my heart to God; and on the other hand, that God only could turn my heart to himself; that it was my duty to love and serve him, but that I could not do this while still unconverted; that it was my duty to pray to him, but that my prayers were a mockery and hateful in his sight; that it was my duty to be good, and I deserved eternal death for not being good; and yet that I was as powerless to make myself good, as is the Ethiopian to change the color of his skin. Now, it is perfectly useless to teach children such contradictory doctrines: they are not metaphysicians, and will not attempt to reconcile them; if they believe one, they will not believe the other. That my nature was utterly corrupt; that I was incapable of doing one holy act; that it was impossible for a holy God to view me with any complacency, and equally impossible for me to change this evil nature—these things had been constantly preached to me from my earliest days. It was a waste of words, therefore, to tell me that I ought to love God, and deserved punishment for not loving him and doing his will. Every child knows that he is not to blame for not doing what he cannot do. This principle comes into exercise in all the actions of his daily life, and he applies the same principle to the duties which God requires of him. He will *say* he is a sinner for not doing some impossible thing, if he thinks his parents expect him to say so; but he will feel no compunctions of conscience on account of his deficiencies. Having lived through my second revival without being converted, I made no objection to the statement that I had been all the time striving against the Holy Spirit, and that it would now be perfectly right, and just what might be expected, if God should abandon me to my own chosen courses; yet I had no sense of ill-desert in reflecting upon the matter, and never believed God would finally leave me to perish.

When a person, whose feelings on religious subjects have been aroused during one of these "revivals," passes through it without "experiencing religion," he is expected to fall back into his former state of unconcern, and to become even a greater sinner than before; he has wilfully rejected the proffered mercy; he has turned a deaf ear to the voice of the Saviour; he has trampled in the dust the precious blood shed for his redemption; he has come to the door of the sanctuary and turned his back upon it; he returns "as a dog to his vomit, and as the sow that is washed to her wallowing in the mire." After all this, what hope is there of his final salvation? "Ephraim is joined to his idols, let him alone," is the consoling text which his kind friends are never weary of repeating in his ears.

It seems strange that real conversions ever occur under such a system of instruction as I have described; and the fact is only to be explained by supposing that in most cases God takes compassion upon the ignorance of his suffering creatures, and gives them some unusual sense of relief or satisfaction, or some more vivid perception of his attributes than they have had before, or even some peculiar bodily sensation will answer the purpose; anything which they can seize upon as affording the least ground of hope that they have "met with the change" for which they have been longing. This hope, however slight it may be, gives rise to a corresponding degree of joy and thankfulness, and these emotions, being regarded as the very best evidence of conversion, increase the hope to confidence and exultation, and the convert is welcomed into the company of Christ's chosen ones. Snatched from the eternal misery to which he was hastening, and having his salvation secured beyond the possibility of losing it, then, and not till then, does he resolve, trusting in the grace of God for assistance, to live henceforth a Christian life; for he has always been taught that he must be converted before it is possible to make such a resolution with sincerity.

An interval of five years now passed, during

which, so far as I remember, the duty of personal piety was never suggested to me by any one. I attended prayers morning and evening at the chapel, after entering college, and on Sunday went to church twice; but here all my religious exercises ended. I did not even pray to God privately, considering it of no use. I constantly heard the doctrine taught that every action, even the prayer, of the unconverted man is wholly sinful, an abomination in the sight of God; so I made none.

The next "revival" to the influence of which I was subjected occurred when I was nineteen years old, and a member of the junior class in Yale College. Here, at length, I was, or imagined myself to be, converted. I had learned nothing new in regard to the philosophy of the change. and when the religious excitement made its appearance among the students, and my own hopes were aroused that I might now become a Christian, I could do nothing but have recourse to my old prayers and holy books and pious conversations. How long I had continued in this way, seeing others daily "rejoicing in hope" around me and myself still passed by, I do not remember. But, one day, after having wearied myself out with praying and weeping and dejection, my mental excitement suddenly gave way, and a sort of apathy came over me, so that I felt indifferent tc everything about me. It was a purely physical phenomenon, resulting from nothing but exhaustion, such as I have experienced hundreds of times since; but it was sufficient for my necessities; it aroused a hope that I was converted, and the hope gave me joy and a sense of complacency toward God and my fellow-creatures, which emotions increased the hope and were increased by it, each mutually adding to the other until all my anxiety vanished. My confidence was also sustained by my pious friends, to whom I gave an account of my feelings, and who regarded my sudden change from despondency to rejoicing as in the highest degree satisfactory. I came near losing my hope, however, as suddenly as I had found it; for, having gone out to walk, I soon discovered that my unusual experience had vanished, and that I was feeling just as I always did. I went to Dr. T——, and told him my happy sensations had all left me, and I was afraid I had been deceiving myself; but he replied in such a way as to encourage me, and when I found he considered my state as satisfactory, I regained my confidence, and with it my rejoicing. Then I did what I ought to have done in the first place, but what no one ever intimated to me that I should do—resolve henceforth to serve God and keep his command-ments. If I had not supposed myself converted, I should certainly have made no such resolve, and nobody, so far as I know, would have recommended it; for all would have believed such advice could result in nothing better than a life of hypocrisy and external morality. But for the peculiar physical sensation from which I derived my hope, I should sooner or later have got over my excitement, as in previous instances, from mere inability to keep it up, and relapsed into increased forgetfulness of God and of my duties to him, utterly ignorant of the fact that, in rendering me willing to become a Christian, the Holy Spirit had done all which he could do; that, so far as the work of God was concerned, I was converted from the moment when I experienced this willingness, and that nothing was necessary but that I should stay so.

I have no doubt there are multitudes of persons, brought up as I have been in the doctrines of New England theology, who go through life longing to be Christians and waiting to experience this mysterious change called conversion, in order that they may publicly profess their faith in Christ and join the ranks of his declared disciples, and who are stigmatized as good moral people and nothing more, but who will find, when the light of another world opens upon them, that they have been Christians all their lives without knowing it. And there are multitudes of others who are plunged back into lives of sin, because, when they were ready and anxious to enter the fold of Christ, their pious friends shut them out until they should experience some strange ecstatic emotion for which they waited and prayed in vain. These doctrines would be ludicrous, if the sense of their ludicrousness were not swallowed up in horror of their consequences.

My conversion being regarded as genuine, in due time I joined the college church. In so doing, I stood with others in the centre aisle of the chapel and declared my belief in certain articles of faith, but what they were I do not now know, and doubt whether I knew then. I took it for granted they were all right, and the idea was never suggested to me that it would be well to know beforehand what I was going to adopt as my confession of faith. Such a suggestion would imply that either I myself, or some one else, considered it possible that I could be a Christian, and yet not believe just what my church believed. This was a possibility that certainly did not occur to me. I had been brought up to receive as true precisely what my religious teachers had agreed upon as truth, and did so most implicitly, without a thought of questioning its correctness. It is in this way that almost every one who joins a Congregational church has his creed fixed upon him. The new convert is expected, as a matter of course, to unite with the church to which his parents or friends belong, or which he has been in the habit of attending; and in nine cases out of ten he does not know, until he stands up to give his assent to them, what the doctrines are in which he is solemnly to declare his belief, and in very few instances, probably, does he know much better afterward. If a young person, as most converts are, he may have heard this "confession of faith" read a hundred times without ever having thought of its meaning; and when he declares his acceptance of it, he understands the act as being merely a pledge on his part to live a Christian life, *and* to believe whatever his church and minister say is gospel truth.

After leaving college I was sent by those who had the direction of my education to the theological seminary at Princeton, to be prepared for the ministry. If I was consulted at all in relation to the matter, I have forgotten it; and, though now twenty years old, I had never thought of setting up my own will in opposition to that of my guardians and counsellors. I presume I was sent to Princeton in order that I might enter upon my work thoroughly imbued with the doctrines of Presbyterianism. I knew absolutely nothing in regard to the differences of opinion among the various sects calling themselves "orthodox," and supposed they all held very nearly the same doctrines. I went to the theological school, that I might learn what to believe myself and to preach in future to others, and expected to believe whatever might be taught me, just as I had been accustomed to accept the facts of natural science as explained by my college teachers. That I had a right to take the Bible for my sole guide, and to form my opinions as to its doctrines independent of and in opposition to those of the theological professor, certainly never occurred to me; and if I had broached such a heresy, I should have been dismissed without ceremony. During the first year of my theological course, I was engaged chiefly in the study of Hebrew, and had little to do with doctrines. In the second year, however, I found a constant conflict going on in my own mind between what seemed the dictates of common sense, and the necessity of receiving as God's truth the dogmas promulgated by the professors. I was beginning to think for myself, and could not understand why Christianity should require me to believe, not only so many things beyond my comprehension—this I expected—but so much which seemed inconsistent with the natural sense of right and wrong which God himself had created within me. I found it totally impossible to believe some of these dogmas without assuming that my natural instincts had become so depraved that I could not tell good from evil. But as my own moral sense must direct my own actions, I must depend upon its decisions or be left to wander in utter darkness. As, however, I still supposed that the doctrines which were taught were those of the Bible, I could not reject the former without at the same time losing my faith in the latter.

I next began to reflect upon the circumstances and character of my supposed conversion. I still retained the idea that it was the doctrine of my church that in conversion such a supernatural change is wrought in the subject of it, that his tastes and feelings all become different from what they were before; that he afterward will not only avoid whatever is sinful, but will have no disposition to sin; that he will not only resist his evil inclinations, but will have few or none to resist. But in examining myself, I soon became satisfied that no such change had taken place in me. My likes and dislikes were the same as they had been before I was converted. I had no taste for vicious habits, and had never had; I preferred good to evil, as a gene ral rule, but so I had always done. I read pious books from a sense of duty, but found a pleasant story far more interesting. I attended prayer-meetings for the same reason, but often found them very tiresome, and enjoyed a game of chess or back gammon much more. I assumed a sedate deportment, as became a student of divinity, but envied the undergradates of Nassau Hall their noisy sports. In a word, I was the same man, or boy more properly, that I had always been. Then, in reflecting upon the manner of my conversion, I came to the conclusion that I had, by my own imagination, made a "change of heart" out of a giddiness of head, and that my supposed "new birth" was nothing but a creation of my own fancy. I knew that I had, in general, been endeavoring to do my duty toward God and my fellow-creatures, and that my attempts had been very unsuccessful; but I also knew that I had been making the attempt only because I supposed myself to be converted; for it was still an article of my creed, as I understood it, that an unconverted man cannot love and serve God, and therefore there is no use in his trying to do so.

I next transferred my observation to my fellow-students, and soon became convinced they were no more changed than myself; and carrying my investigations out among the pious people whom I knew or had known, and reflecting upon the many exhibitions which I had seen in them of tastes and feelings and passions which seemed to me wrong and un-Christian, my conviction became gradually fixed that this notion of conversion was wholly a delusion. But this was tearing out the very cornerstone of the whole system of doctrine in which I had been educated, and it is not to be wondered at that the entire structure soon tumbled into ruins. The result was, that I declared my loss of all faith in the Christian religion, which declaration, of course, put an end to my theological studies.

Dr. W——, through whose influence I had probably been sent to Princeton, took me away and kept me for a week at his house in B——, attempting no argument with me, but wanting me to read the Bible all the time. What he expected this would effect I cannot imagine; for I had been reading the Bible all my life and had never found out that Calvinism and Christianity are not identical terms.

That in renouncing my faith in the religion of the Bible, I was actuated by no desire to free myself from the obligation of living a virtuous life is evident, I think, from the fact that my conduct was as strictly moral afterward as before. I never for a moment doubted that there was a God who was good and holy, and who required goodness and holiness in his creatures, and whom it was my duty to please; and to this God, whom I recognized in his works and in the government of the world, I continued to address my prayers. It was only the religion revealed in the Scriptures which I rejected.

I cannot give a detailed account of my religious feelings and opinions during the next ten years, the last eight of which, as you know, were spent in wandering about the world, far from home. I never made any open manifestation of infidelity, and always respected the religious sentiments of others; and, so far as I know, none of the persons with whom I was associated ever knew that I called myself a sceptic. They considered me merely a man professing to be governed by moral principle, but, like themselves, belonging to no church.

During the last two or three years of this period, I became more and more dissatisfied with my situation. I began by thinking that there might, after all, be some truth in this religion which I was rejecting, and if so, I was in a very unsafe position; for I was liable at any time to die in my unbelief. Such thoughts were only occasional, occurring at longer or shorter intervals, and it is now impossible for me to recall anything definite in regard to them or their gradual action upon my mind. I only know that they resulted in my resuming the faith which I had cast off. The evidences of the truth of the divine revelation by slow degrees so pressed themselves upon me, that I was compelled to yield to their force. The argument which had the greatest weight with me, and which seemed quite unanswerable, was this: and I beg you to remember it, for I shall have occasion to refer to it hereafter. I found the religion of the cross, claiming to have come down to us from the days of certain men who had founded it and given their lives for it, and who had established certain rites called sacraments, which had been practised from the very commencement, by those professing a belief in the religion. Now, either this system of religion, with its external and obligatory rites, was established at the time at which it was said to have been, or at some subsequent time rational people were persuaded to believe that a new religion, which neither they nor any of their countrymen had ever before heard of, was no novelty at all; that they and their fathers before them had always been taught it; that they and their fathers had been practising the rites of baptism and the Lord's Supper, in commemoration of certain events in the life of the founder of this religion, though they knew perfectly well that they had never before heard of any of these things. Such a supposition is so obviously absurd, that no person of ordinary intelligence can accept it. This religion, therefore, must have been established at the time and by the men at which and by whom it professes to have been, or it could not have come into existence at all. But the first believers in the religion must have had a personal knowledge of the men called apostles, and must have known that they believed what they were teaching, and that they proved their belief by dying for the sake of it. In the third place, that all these men could be deceived in regard to the character of their master, with whom they had been in constant intercourse for years, and in regard to the genuineness of the miracles by which he proved his divine mission, would have been the greatest miracle on record. This rendered the chain of evidence complete and irrefragable.

I had been thus logically compelled to admit the historical truth of the Scriptures and the divine origin of the religion taught in them, for more than a year before I made known to any one my change of views. My reasoning was, that, in order to be a Christian, there was no necessity of joining a church. I regarded all churches as merely associations of believers, holding the fundamental doctrines of the New Testament, indeed, but interpreting them each according to its own fancy, and requiring that their members, as a condition of membership, should subscribe beforehand to views prepared for them by men who had no authority whatever to prescribe to others what they should believe and profess. But, as it would have been useless for me to call myself a Christian while refusing to join any church, I made no profession of faith in the religion of Christ. By taking this course, I shut myself out from the Lord's Supper; but this, I argued, was not my fault; it was chargeable upon those who refused me access to the Lord's table unless I would agree to believe just what they chose to require, however false or absurd it might appear to me. I regarded the sacrament, also, as it is commonly regarded by Protestants, as having no virtue in itself; as being nothing more than a ceremony designed to keep in memory the death of our Lord, and affording a means by which Christians may periodically make a public profession of their faith in him. Viewing it in this light, I considered a participation in it as of no very essential importance.

I doubt, however, whether I ever felt quite satisfied with this position, and at length, in the summer of 184–, thirteen years after my renunciation of the Christian religion at Princeton, I determined to resume publicly the faith which I had then cast off. I was forced to admit the duty of confessing with the lips, as well as believing with the heart, that Jesus is the Christ, the Son of God. I was also convinced that a public profession of my faith in him was absolutely necessary as a safeguard against the temptations to sin to which I was constantly exposed, and that it was a mistake to suppose that I could be a consistent Christian without letting any one know it. But the steps by which I was brought to this conclusion were so gradual that I can fix upon no particular point of time at which my mind was exercised in any unusual degree in regard to these matters.

Having thus decided to reunite myself with the "visible church," it became a question with me, With what branch of it shall I connect myself?

I had, for many years, been in the habit of attending the Episcopal Church, and preferred the service as there performed; but I had been born and brought up among Congregationalists, and nearly all my relatives belonged to that communion. I presumed, also, that I myself was still a member, under discipline, of the college church where I had made my first profession. Just at this time, moreover, *Neal's History of the Puritans* happened to fall into my hands, in reading which I became so disgusted with the horrible persecutions to which he represents these people as being subjected by the Church of England, that I concluded this could not be the Church of Christ, and that I must look for it elsewhere. The result was, that I wrote to New Haven, acknowledging my errors, and asking a dismission from the college church and a recommendation to that of —— in B——, where I was then residing. My application was favorably received and answered, Dr. —— saying that my case was by no means a new one; that he had had many such; which is not to be wondered at, when one considers how many of those who are received into the college church are mere boys, who have never begun to reason for themselves in regard to anything of more importance than the color of a coat or the fit of a pair of boots.

I took my letters to Dr. ——, who had already been made acquainted with the particulars of my case, appeared before the examining committee, who said nothing to me that I remember, and in due time was received into fellowship as a member of the —— church of B——. One question put to me by Dr. ——, and my reply to it, remain fixed in my memory. He asked me whether I ever had a recurrence of my doubts. My answer was, that I had, but that I had determined not to listen to them. This answer expresses the state of my mind at that time. I had decided that the Christian religion is true and divine, and had resolved to accept and live by it. But when some of the doctrines which appeared to be taught by it presented themselves alone to my acceptance, my faith was staggered by them, and it required a vigorous effort of the will to say, as I did say, If this is Christian doctrine, I will believe it if I can; and if I cannot believe it, I will not let it disturb my trust in God's wisdom and goodness as revealed in Jesus Christ.

When I was received into communion with the —— church, I did the same thing which I had done sixteen years before at New Haven; that is, I stood up and publicly professed my acceptance of certain "Articles of Faith," without knowing what they were until I heard them read. I did this, however, with very different purposes from those which I had then had. Then, as I have already said, I regarded it as a duty to acknowledge as truth whatever my church might teach. Now, I had no such idea. I considered it necessary to unite myself with a Christian church, and in order to do so I was compelled to acquiesce in the "Articles of Faith" agreed upon by its members and minister; but in assenting to them I did not consider myself bound by them for one moment longer than I was myself satisfied of their truth. I had not, for so many years, denied the authority of even the Apostle Paul in order now to fall back into an admission of that of a modern church committee, or of any uninspired man or body of men, of the present or any antecedent age. "The Bible alone" was assumed by me, not theoretically merely, but practically, as my rule of faith, and I claimed that it was not only my right, but my duty, to examine every doctrine for myself in the light of God's word, and to accept or reject it according to my own judgment as to its truth, regardless of the opinions of others who had no better authority than myself to pronounce upon it. I had found out that John Calvin had no more right to decide what my faith should be than had Martin Luther; the Synod of Dort than the Westminster Assembly; Dr. —— at Princeton than Dr. —— at New Haven; that very different views were held and taught by different theologians; that the creed of a church is generally that of its minister, and his that of the school at which he was educated; and that all these different views and different creeds represented nothing but the opinions of men who made no claim whatever to any divine authority to teach divine truth. Therefore, as, among these contradictory opinions, many must necessarily be false, my only rational course was to accept none of them unconditionally until I should myself be convinced that they were taught in the Bible.

It was at this time that I decided on resuming the purpose which had been interrupted so many years before, of entering the Christian ministry, and that I went to Andover for the completion of the theological studies that had been begun at Princeton. I carried to Andover my independence of the judgment of other men, and during my course of study there, while listening attentively to the instructions of the professor of theology, felt under no obligation to accept the truth of all his doctrines, unless I was satisfied with his reasoning and his evidence.

Some men—perhaps most men—acting on the principle by which I was governed, would have gradually built up a system of faith for themselves out of a mass of probabilities, and having once formed it, would, by mere force of will, refusing to see anything that opposed their opinions, have eventually persuaded themselves that there could be no doubt in regard to the correctness of their views. If I had been ten years younger, I might have done so myself. The actual result in my case, however, was very different. Among the conflicting doctrines taught by different schools, I found it impossible to come to any more satisfactory decision than that some seemed to be true and others to be false; while there were very few with regard to which I could venture to express an opinion, with absolute certainty that it was correct. My creed came to be nothing but a collection of opinions held with various degrees of confidence, but containing almost no articles to which I could say "credo," "I believe," without any mental reservation whatever. As for the attempts which I heard made to explain the doctrines of the Bible, many of them seemed to me very unsatisfactory, and some utterly absurd; so that I came to the conclusion, and often said, that ministers involve themselves in inextricable difficulties by trying to know too much, and that it would be far better for them frankly to acknowledge their ignorance of many things, in pretending to explain which to their people they only stultify themselves.

It will be seen at once, that when I had completed my course of theological study, and was licensed to preach, I was totally unqualified to assume the spiritual charge of a congregation of men and women who might reasonably expect me to instruct them as to what they should receive as religious truth. I could tell them what I myself believed, or thought I did; but if any person had asked me, "Do you think it necessary for me to believe as you do, in order to be saved?" I should have been obliged to reply, "I do not know."

I will endeavor to state, so far as I can recall them, the main articles of my creed at this time. I received the Bible as the inspired word of God, though I was unable to decide in what sense, or to what extent, it was written by divine inspiration. This question is an unsettled one in the schools, and it was useless for me to attempt to settle it. I believed that the "Bible alone is a sufficient rule of faith," because, on any other supposition, there seemed to be no rule at all. I also believed that every one must decide for himself as to what the teachings of the Bible are, for the manifest reason that no authority now exists by which these teachings are to be explained. The Apostles, and possibly some of their immediate successors, spoke by inspiration, and their words are to be received as the voice of God; but for certainly fifteen hundred years this voice has been silent, and during this time no man has been so commissioned to preach the Gospel as to render obedience to his instructions obligatory upon me or any one else. The *dicta* of those who have assumed to act as teachers, and who have been followed by large masses of disciples, are nothing but opinions, binding upon no one. Some of these opinions are probably true, but the far larger number must necessarily be false, hence, among these conflicting doctrines, every man must judge for himself which are to be received and which rejected; for in adopting any of them blindly he is quite as likely to believe error as truth. His rule is, and must be, the Bible as he understands it; for the moment he is required to adopt the opinions of others in opposition to his own, he is compelled to admit that the Bible alone is not a sufficient "rule of faith" for him, however sufficient it may be for others.

Now, if the Scriptures contain the rules of action by which God requires me to regulate my life, and the articles of faith which he requires me to believe, and if he has given me no infallible guide in the interpretation of his law, while threatening me with eternal punishment in case I fail to act and believe in accordance with his will, it is impossible to avoid the conviction that he has so expressed that will as to render it perfectly intelligible to every one who sincerely wishes to know and to do it. On any other supposition, God may punish me hereafter for having neglected to obey a command, the existence of which was not only unknown to me, but even impossible to be known. Such a doctrine seems so monstrous, so utterly at variance with every idea of justice, that I have always doubted either the sense or the sincerity of its defenders. I have heard it argued that since human laws do not admit the plea of ignorance as an excuse for transgression, divine justice is not required to do it. But the argument is a very weak one. The human judge must assume that all men are acquainted with laws properly promulgated, because, in each particular case, he has no means of ascertaining whether the ignorance alleged by the culprit under trial is real or pretended, and if the former, whether it is voluntary or involuntary, excusable or inexcusable. Moreover, no judge or jury would condemn a man for transgressing a law which was so obscurely worded that a dozen different interpretations could honestly be put upon it. If the accused could show that he had obeyed the law as he understood it, and that his interpretation of it might possibly be the true one, the sense of justice of the whole community would demand his acquittal. He had merely made a mistake into which, under such a law, the most law-abiding citizen might fall ; and if such a mistake deserved punishment, no one could feel secure.

Applying this plain principle of justice to the law of God, he has certainly so declared his will that his creatures can understand it, or they must be excused for not obeying it; but if the divine law is so clearly expressed, that all who desire to do so can understand it, how comes it that so many and such conflicting interpretations are put upon it?

Many a confident, self-satisfied sectarian will reply at once, "It is because men do not wish to know the truth, and persistently shut their eyes to it." In many cases this may very possibly be the reason; but, on the other hand, in very many others it does not seem to be. Suppose, distrusting my own unaided judgment, and desiring to settle the articles of my faith in a satisfactory manner, I have invited half a dozen men of as many different persuasions to discuss with me the points of doctrine in regard to which they disagree. So far as I can judge, all are equally intelligent, equally devout, equally sincere, and equally confident in the soundness of their own opinions; and no one can doubt that such persons may easily be found in every denomination of Christians. They all declare that they have formed their opinions upon a careful and prayerful examination of the word of God, and anxious only to know the truth. Yet no two have come to the same conclusion. Am I to infer from this that only one of the six really desires this knowledge, and that the other five are hypocrites? This would be a very uncharitable inference. But even supposing this to be the true explanation of their differences, of what use is it to me unless I can ascertain which of the whole number is the true seeker after truth? I can discover no marks by which to distinguish the genuine coin from the counterfeit; all have the same weight, the same ring, the same stamp. How can I make an intelligent choice among them? And suppose, after having heard all which each man can say in defence of his position, I should decide to adopt the opinions of one and reject those of the others, how can I be sure that I have not made a mistake? My opinion is worth no more, because it is mine, than it would be if it were another man's. It is of more importance to me, because I must act upon it; but absolutely, in deciding what is true and what is false, it is merely the opinion of one man, and of very little value. If, after having formed it, I were to insist that it must necessarily be correct, and that only their own unwillingness to know and believe the truth prevents all other persons from seeing it as I do, I should justly be regarded as a self-conceited fool, whose judgment was of no value whatever. My decision is my opinion, and nothing else or more, and plainly decides nothing beyond my own actions. I may, therefore, be wrong, after all my attempts to find the truth, and in condemning those who fail to discover it, I should be in great danger of passing sentence upon myself.

I have often heard it said that they who pray for the guidance of the Holy Spirit, in their search after truth, and trust themselves unreservedly to that guidance, will never be led into error. But the man who urges this in defence of his own opinions, merely assumes, in the face of abundant evidence to the contrary, that only he, and those who agree with him, have—or think they have—prayed for such guidance in a right frame of mind, while all others have neglected to do so. That the proposition, as stated, is true, there is no need of denying. It is enough to say that a man may mistake in judging his own feelings and emotions, as easily as in judging any thing else. Or he may sincerely desire to be taught of God in some things, while in others he prefers to act upon his own judgment; and he who asks for divine guidance in regard to one matter, while rejecting it in relation to another, can have no reason to complain, if left altogether to his own wisdom.

In view of the foregoing considerations, I saw no means of avoiding one or the other of two conclusions. On the one hand, God has given his creatures a law so vaguely expressed that, with a sincere desire to understand it, many of them fail to do so, at the same time threatening with the most fearful penalties every transgression of that law; or, on the other, the matters with regard to which there is such a conflict of opinions are unessential, and no evil will result from leaving them undecided. The first proposition seemed too monstrous for belief; I was, therefore, compelled to adopt the second, and this became a fundamental article of my creed, as I think it is of the creed of Protestants generally.

But when I attempted to draw the dividing line between essentials and non-essentials, I found myself quite unable to do so. It was easy enough to decide that the points of doctrine which are made matters of dispute in the various trinitarian or, so called, "orthodox" sects, belong to the latter class; also, questions in regard to church government, the time and mode of administering baptism, and so forth. But in the course of my life I had known intimately large numbers of persons calling themselves Unitarians, who, so far as I was able to judge, were as sincere in their faith and as exemplary in their lives as the members of any "orthodox" church. They believe that Jesus Christ is the "Saviour," the "Messiah," the "Son of God," everything that he can be except God. How could I be certain they were living in an error which would plunge them into eternal death, when I could not doubt that they meant to believe in the Bible, and denied the divinity of our Lord only because they honestly thought the doctrine is not taught there? It is impossible to doubt the sincerity of these persons and their perfect confidence in the correctness of their belief; for they prove both by being willing to die and appear before the bar of God, trusting in his promises as they understand them. Many of them also are men who are admired for their learning and wisdom and scholarship, and who have made the Bible and its doctrines the study of their lives. Yet they do not believe that Jesus Christ is "Very God." What am I to infer from this? Applying my previous reasoning to this case, it would run thus: Whatever God requires his creatures to believe, he has stated so plainly that all who will may know it; many persons who, so far as I have the means of judging, do wish to know the truth, fail to find this doctrine taught in the Bible; the logical inference is, it is not so taught as it would be if a belief in it were necessary to salvation, and it must be classed among the non-essentials. But can this be possible? Either I am guilty of exalting a creature to the throne of God, and giving him the worship and homage which belong to God alone ; or they who reject the doctrine are guilty of dragging the Almighty from his seat, and degrading him to the level of his own creatures. Can he view either of these monstrous sins as an excusable error, resulting from a misunderstanding of his written word? That Christ is God seems to me to be taught in the Bible ; but I can easily understand how a person brought up in the Unitarian church should be unable to put any other interpretation upon the doctrine of the Trinity, than that there are three supreme Gods, equal in substance, power, and glory. Viewing it in this light, he must reject it or renounce his reason. Moreover, if the doctrine of the divinity of Christ is so plainly taught in the Scripture as many persons suppose, what has been the necessity of writing so many books in order to prove it, age after age, from the days of Arius down to the present time? A doctrine which requires so much to be said in its defence certainly admits of much being said against it. Is it, then, or is it not, one of the doctrines which may be safely left undecided ; does it, or does it not, belong to the class of non-essentials? At the time of which I am now writing, I was unable to answer this question in any other way than by saying, "I do not know."

But if it is of no essential importance whether

Jesus Christ is regarded as God or as one of his creatures, the views which may be adopted by different individuals in regard to his person and the nature of his mission, must be of no consequence whatever; for the interval existing between the highest and lowest created beings vanishes into nothing, when compared with that which exists between the Supreme Jehovah and the most exalted of his creatures. Whether, therefore, I consider the Messiah to have been far above the loftiest archangel or only a man like Moses and Joshua, is scarcely worth asking or answering. What my opinion may be with regard to his object in coming to the earth and the end attained by his living and dying here, is quite immaterial. But if this be so, is there any doctrine of the Bible which different persons may not safely understand in different ways? Is there any doctrine so explicitly stated that it may not be variously interpreted? Again, if we may believe whatever seems to us to be taught in the Bible, and be safe in that belief, may we not use our reason in the same way in judging of the book itself? May we not doubt its divine authority altogether? Much may be and has been said and written to prove it to be purely a human composition. If our intellects should be convinced that it is nothing else—if we fail to see the evidences of its divine origin—can we justly be condemned for an honest error in judgment, so long as we sincerely desire to know the truth and to do the will of Almighty God?

You see the end to which my reasoning has brought me. I started with the proposition, that God has given his creatures the means of learning infallibly all which he requires they should believe. This is undeniably true. I have ended with the consequence, that it is of no importance what they believe or disbelieve, so long as they are sincere and virtuous. This is just as undeniably false. But at what point in the argument did the reasoning cease to be true and begin to be false? This is a question which, with no other teacher than the Bible, I have never been able to answer. That I was required to believe something, did not admit of a doubt. Our Saviour has said: "He that believeth shall be saved; he that believeth not shall be damned." There is no mistaking these words, at all events; they are as plain as language can make them; but, believeth what? As originally spoken, the meaning of the words is perfectly clear. Our Lord was addressing the eleven apostles: "Go ye into all the world, and preach the gospel to every creature: he that believeth *your preaching*, and is baptized, shall be saved; he that believeth *it* not shall be damned." There is no difficulty here;

any who might fail to understand the preaching of an apostle could obtain an explanation from his own lips, and he could adapt that explanation to every man's capacity. But what am I to do now, when conscious of my inability to understand what it is which I am required to believe? The apostles have all been dead for nearly eighteen hundred years; no person is now living having authority to explain the few letters and annals which they have left behind. They have not even given a formal draft of the creed which I am required to accept, and I am obliged to pick it out from their writings, and piece it together for myself to the best of my ability. Some things I feel sure are positively stated; some seem to be taught in one place while in another I find statements that appear to conflict with them; some are so obscurely hinted at, that I can form no clear idea of their meaning; and yet this terrible threat hangs over my head, "Believe, or be damned." What can I do but cry out, almost in despair: "Lord, what must I believe? I cannot understand the book, and there is no Philip here to explain it to me."

It is probable that you will fail to comprehend my perplexity, because you have never had a doubt as to what you are to believe, and you have always regarded your own faith as derived by yourself from the Bible. But I think a very little reflection will convince you that this is a mistake. You were taught what you now believe by your parents and friends long before you were old enough to read the Bible understandingly, and you implicitly received as true just what you were taught, and have never for a moment harbored the thought that these teachings might be erroneous; you would have been shocked had you ever found a doubt in regard to their correctness springing up in your mind, and would have regarded as a religious duty its immediate suppression. But the fact that you have been educated in one system of doctrine and not in another is purely accidental, so far as any events are over which we have no control. It has resulted simply from your having been born in one family, and not in another; in one church, and not in another. If your parents had been Lutheran, or Methodist, or Baptist, or Unitarian, you would have grown up with just as firm a conviction of the truth of their doctrines, and you would have found those doctrines just as plainly taught in the Bible, and you would have then been just as much astonished as you now are, if I had been unable to see them so clearly as yourself. There can be no doubt of this whatever, unless you have some reason for supposing that you would have proved the one exception in a thousand to the general rule.

Now try to imagine yourself in the position which I occupied when I regained my faith in revealed religion. I had no creed ready made which it was only necessary for me to take up and carry along. I had the Bible, nothing else. This I regarded as the word of God, from which alone I was to learn his will, and from which alone my faith was to be derived. The world was full of contradictory treatises on Scripture doctrine; but they were all written by men who neither had, nor pretended to have, any right to speak authoritatively. Of those who were once regarded as little less than inspired, some are now thrust aside with contempt, and others have sunk into utter oblivion. Evidently, these mere human expounders of the sacred writings were very unsafe guides, and I could not venture blindly to follow any of them. The same might be said with equal or stronger emphasis in regard to any living teachers. I might listen to their teachings, but could adopt them as articles of faith only when convinced of their truth. But these teachings are as multifarious and conflicting as are the opinions of men on any doubtful subject. What one learned and pious professor reveres as divine truth, another ridicules as sheer nonsense, and a third repels with holy horror as rank heresy. In deciding among these various opinions, I had no guide but the Bible, and whatever point of doctrine might be accepted by me as true, I would be sure to find other men battling against as false, and just as ready as myself to prove from the Bible the correctness of their opinion. Finding, therefore, that every form of doctrine can be established from the Bible to the entire satisfaction of those who hold it, is it strange that the only conclusion to which I could come in regard to all except a few fundamental articles of faith, was, "I do not know what to believe"? I might think the balance of evidence was in favor of one doctrine and against another, and therefore decide to accept the former and reject the latter; but in so doing I was compelled to admit that I might be wrong. I wanted *knowledge* of the truth, not a mere balance of probabilities, and I saw no possible means of ever acquiring it.

Perhaps you will say, this state of doubt and uncertainty was a natural consequence of my having for a time abandoned all faith in the gospel of Christ, and that, but for this, I should have gone on peacefully, believing as I had believed before, and as you believe now. This is very possible; but whether it would have been best for me to do so depends entirely upon whether what I then believed and what you now believe is the exact truth, and that is the very thing in regard to which we may not agree. I presume you will not deny that it is better to be harassed with doubts than to be at rest in error; better not to know what road to take, than to walk confidently in the wrong one.

Or you may say, my troubles arose from my having despised the instructions of others and trusted to my own wisdom for guidance. But in whose wisdom should I trust? I was willing to be taught, but I must know that my teachers possessed the requisite qualifications. Who taught them? and who taught their teachers? Follow the line back, and you will find at the starting-point nothing but human opinion, worth just as much less than the opinions of to-day as the world has advanced in knowledge. The opinions of John Calvin are of little value in comparison with those of living theologians, and there are probably now but few persons who agree with him in all things, though his name was the orthodox shibboleth when we were children. It is easy to say I should trust in the judgment of wise and good men, rather than in my own. Such generalities do not meet the difficulty. Tell me who they are; name them; then go and ask them whether they would advise me or any one to adopt their opinions on all points blindly, and whether they are willing to take the responsibility in case any of those opinions should prove to be erroneous. If they are the wise and good men that you think them to be, they would be appalled at such a proposition.

But in saying what I have supposed you to say, you would admit that a man can secure himself against doubt only by holding fast to the instructions which he has received from others, and not presuming to judge for himself what is taught in the Bible. You would admit the very thing which you probably denied when I asserted it just now; that is, that your faith is fixed and unwavering, not because you have derived it from the Bible, but because you have not. You would admit that he who regards the decisions of other men as mere human opinions, and therefore, possibly erroneous, and who attempts, from the Bible alone, to ascertain what he is required to believe, will almost necessarily find himself involved in perplexity, totally unable to decide what to receive and what to reject. But in admitting this, you abandon at once the Protestant dogma, that the "Bible alone is a sufficient rule of faith;" for a rule of faith which a man cannot safely examine for himself, unless he is already so firmly established in some faith that there is no danger of its being shaken by anything which he may find there, is certainly a very strange one.

The simple fact is, that the Bible is a rule of faith to Protestants to this extent, and no further, that, having received their faith from the oral instruction of their parents and teachers, without the Bible, they have recourse to it in after-years, merely to find in it the things which they have been taught, and which they already believe ; and this they have no difficulty in doing. Now, if they all believed the same thing, and all found it in the Bible, the fact would furnish pretty satisfactory evidence that it is actually there. But how is it to be explained that the most contradictory creeds are found there, to the entire satisfaction of some classes of well-meaning people ? There is evidently something wrong in the practical working of the system ; but what is it?

You must not suppose that this difficulty never occurred to me until I began to examine into the claims of the Catholic Church. I have seen it for twenty years, and have never been able to discover a satisfactory solution of it. I saw that if children are to be taught any religious truth whatever, they must necessarily receive it from their parents and pious friends, by word of mouth, long before they are able to find it for themselves in the Bible. I saw that if the creed of the teachers is false, their errors must as necessarily be absorbed by the mind of the child as is the food which is served out to him by his body; there is no possibility of his escaping this result. I saw that, in some very rare cases, people change their creed in subsequent years; but, as a general rule, so firmly are the doctrines taught in childhood fixed in the mind, that they cannot be eradicated without, at the same time, uprooting all faith in the religion of the Bible, leaving only a blank infidelity in its place, Seeing these things, which seemed to me indisputable facts, I could not avoid asking myself how far those, who, under such circumstances, are believing error instead of truth, are responsible for their errors, and what age or what degree of intelligence is necessary before persons thus brought up in a false system of doctrine can reasonably be expected to discover the fact. I could make no reply to these questions, and was obliged to rest satisfied with the reflection that God knows his own purposes, and will do all things well and wisely — a reflection evidently based, not upon Christianity, but upon natural religion.

But with all these difficulties suggesting themselves to my mind, in opposition to the dogma that the "Bible alone is a sufficient rule of faith,"

I nevertheless retained it as a fundamental article of my creed, because it seemed to me absolutely necessary; I knew of no other "rule," and it must be the Bible or nothing. I had tried the "nothing," and found it would not do.

After what I have already said, it is scarcely necessary for me to add that my creed was made up almost wholly of negations with very few affirmations. I believed that the sin of Adam has entailed upon his descendants a nature which is predisposed to sin. But I did not believe that any man is guilty of the sin of Adam, or exposed to punishment on account of it. The doctrine of the Westminster Assembly's Catechism, that "all men sinned in him," if the words are to be understood in their ordinary signification, seemed to me utterly ridiculous.

I believed that Jesus Christ came to the earth, and suffered and died, in order that mankind might be freed from the consequences of Adam's sin. But I did not believe that he suffered the punishment due to men for their sins, nor that he was punished at all, in any proper sense of the word. I believed the incarnation and sufferings of Christ were necessary, otherwise they would not have taken place; but I did not believe they were necessary because God was unable to pardon a repentant sinner without them, or because he was obliged to inflict upon some person the penalties pronounced against sin. Why they were necessary I did not pretend to know.

My views in relation to future punishment, if I had made them known, would have been regarded by my church as exceedingly unorthodox. I was very doubtful whether any human beings would be made to suffer through all eternity on account of sins committed in this life. I could not see why a God of infinite benevolence would not provide some means of preventing this, if for no other reason than to satisfy his own desire for the happiness of his creatures. That he could derive any positive gratification from witnessing their torments seemed to me a shocking doctrine, and I never accepted it for a moment. None of the attempts which I have seen or heard to reconcile the fact of eternal punishment with his infinite goodness and justice, were satisfactory to my mind. At the same time I was obliged to confess that the fact itself does seem to be taught in the Scriptures so plainly as to render a denial of it almost impossible. I remained, therefore, in a state of unbelief, rather than of positive disbelief, in regard to the doctrine. I hoped it might eventually be found that we misunderstand the teachings of the

Bible, and that God knows how he may fulfil every word which he has spoken, and yet, at some distant day, banish all sin and all suffering from his creation.

The peculiar views, however, which are held by the New England "orthodox" churches in regard to future punishment, I rejected without hesitation. The opinion once sustained by so many, that infants are born into the world with natures so corrupted by sin that, in case of their death, they must be cast at once into hell—that "hell is paved with infants' bones"—this doctrine is so abhorrent to the natural instincts of the human heart that I have never met any one who defended it. But it is still believed by New England Christians that as soon as the child has reached an age at which he is capable of knowing right from wrong, he becomes subject to the same law as his parents, and cannot be saved without going through the process which I have already described, known by the name of "conversion." As, however, this change seldom takes place, or is even looked for, at an earlier age than from twelve to fifteen years, it follows that the vast majority of children who die before this period are sent at once to eternal misery. It matters not how lovely, how amiable, how apparently conscientious they may have been during their brief lives; they died unconverted, and are now suffering the unending torments of hell. Such a doctrine as this I have never believed.

Again, suppose two men to die at the same time; one of them has lived a life of irreproachable integrity; he has been a good husband and father; has endeavored to fulfil his duties toward his fellow-men in all respects, and was the object of the esteem and love of all who knew him; but he never "made a profession of religion," and died unconverted. He is in hell, cast into the company of devils and all vile beings, to abide with them for ever. The other man has spent his whole life in wickedness, having been an outlaw from society, a blasphemer of God, a hater of all good, a robber and a murderer; but an hour before he expiated his crimes upon the gallows, he "experienced a change of heart," and "gave satisfactory evidence" of conversion. He has gone directly to heaven, and in the glorious company of saints and angels is singing the praises of redeeming love. One of these men has never done a good thing in his life, and he is to be for ever blessed. The other has never intentionally done an evil deed, and he is to be for ever damned. This kind of doctrine I have never been able to believe. I felt perfectly sure that the sacred writers never meant to teach it.

Especially does this become incredible when taken in connection with the other "orthodox" dogma, that conversion is not the act of the sinner, but is wholly and solely the gift of God; that the sinner not only does not, but absolutely cannot convert himself. So that in the case supposed above, one of the two men is rewarded with eternal happiness for having done what he did not do; the other is punished with eternal misery for not having done what he could not do. Is it possible for absurdity under the guise of religious truth to go further than this?

The doctrine that the sinner cannot, of his own volition, repent follows logically from the antecedent doctrine that human nature has become totally depraved in consequence of the sin of our first parents. If the nature of man is wholly evil, it is as useless to expect it to produce any right emotions, as it would be to look for grapes in a bramble bush. "An evil tree cannot bring forth good fruit." Before the bramble can produce grapes, it must be changed into a vine; but there is no point in it, from the lowermost root to the topmost twig, where the first initial step in such a process of change can begin. It is a bramble by nature, and can germinate into nothing but brambles. I need not say that this doctrine of total depravity formed no part of my creed.

I believed in the necessity of regeneration; but I supposed this change to be identical with conversion, for so I had always been taught. Conversion I believed to consist in a change of purpose in the sinner; in a resolution, with God's assistance, to renounce all sin, and to obey in the future the divine commandments; this I regarded as the whole of it; and this I believed the sinner can resolve and can begin to do whenever he pleases, without waiting to pray or to read a chapter in the Bible or to do anything else. At the same time, I believed that no man does make this resolve unless impelled to it by the direct influences of the Holy Spirit upon his mind, though he is perfectly able to do it without any such impulse if he chooses.

The sacraments of the church I regarded as they are commonly regarded by members of the communion to which I belonged. Baptism I considered to be nothing but a ceremony by which parents publicly profess their intention to bring up their children in the fear of the Lord, and by which adults unite themselves to the external church. The Lord's Supper I looked upon as a mere memorial of the death of the Saviour. I did not suppose that either of the sacraments has any virtue in itself, or changes in the slightest degree the condition or state of the recipient. It follows, of course, that I considered them of no very essential importance.

The bodies which Protestants call churches, I regarded as nothing more than a union into one external company of persons who hold, or profess to hold, the same religious opinions, in order that they may worship together. I did not recognize the right of such a body to prescribe to me or to any one what we must believe, and I disapproved the practice which is almost universal, of incorporating into their "confession of faith" the peculiar views which they may hold in regard to points of doctrine which are matters of dispute among Christians. I considered this as especially unjustifiable in small country towns where there is usually but one church, as the effect is, either to exclude from church-membership all whose opinions do not precisely coincide with those of the ruling majority, or to compel them to resort to some mental reservation by which to justify themselves in publicly professing to believe things of the truth of which they are by no means satisfied. As the Bible alone is the rule of faith, and as all men have an equal right to judge of its meaning, it follows, as a logical consequence, that all who profess to believe it, and who appear to live Christian lives, should be admitted to the Lord's table. As such a practice as this, however, would probably result in interminable disputes in regard to points of doctrine among members of the same church, I saw that it would be inexpedient and perhaps productive of more evil than the present method, which compels many persons to profess to believe what they do not.

As regards the great mass of the ministers of these churches, I did not think they had any special calling or any special fitness for the position which they occupied. I knew it was a very common idea with young ministers that they had had a call to preach the gospel; but I was convinced this call existed nowhere but in their own imaginations. My reasoning was, that if our Lord had given them any such call, he would have made known to them the truth which they were to preach to others. But unless truth is as multiform as error, very few of them can hold it, and it is impossible to decide which these are among the far larger number who do not. Besides, I was satisfied that most young men go into the ministry for precisely the same purpose for which others engage in the practice of law or medicine; that is, to get a living by it; and if they knew beforehand that they would fail in this, they would regard this fact as furnishing satisfac ory evidence that they had no "call" to the work. There are certainly exceptions; there are some men in the ministry of high talent and general education who might have done vastly better, in a worldly point of view, if they had chosen a different profession, and who have renounced paths that would have led to wealth and preferment from a pure desire to spend their lives in laboring for the conversion of sinners. But these are evidently very exceptional cases, as every one, I think, must acknowledge who will pass in review before his mind all the clergymen whom he knows, and examine them, one by one, in reference to this matter.

There was one question, personal to myself, to which I was unable to give a satisfactory answer. When was I converted? Almost every convert under the New England system knows the precise day and hour when he "met with a change." He can state very minutely what he was doing at the time, of what he was thinking, and what were the feelings which led him to infer that he was "born again." I could have done the same thing during the first three years after my conversion in college; but I came to the conclusion subsequently that my peculiar sensations were wholly physical, and I had never seen any reason to abandon this view of the matter. I have just stated what my opinions now were in regard to the nature of conversion. When, therefore, did it take place in my case? I certainly made the resolution, at the time referred to, that I would abandon sin and obey the divine law, and I endeavored, with varying degrees of constancy and success, to keep it, until I became convinced that my supposed conversion was a delusion. Even after having abandoned my faith in revealed religion, I retained a belief in a supreme God, who had a right to require me, his creature, to do right and to avoid evil, and I think I did act, to some extent at least, in reference to his will. Had I, then, been truly converted while in college, and had I been really a Christian through all the years during which I had been denying my Redeemer? The question seems a very absurd one; but I had never thought of doubting the correctness of the doctrine which I had been taught, that regeneration and conversion are the same thing, and as it is evident that no man can be regenerated twice, if the change did not occur in me at the time specified, I had no idea when it did. The last revolution in my views and feelings was so gradual, that I was not myself conscious of the changes going on in them unless I compared them at long intervals; and at no time, so far as I recollect, was I aroused into anything like a state of religious excitement. I was as calm and deliberate in my reasonings and conclusions as if I had been studying some purely scientific subject, and admitted one truth after another only as I became convinced that it could no longer be doubted. It was impossible to fix upon any particular point of time as the turning-point in my faith. When, therefore, did I "become a Christian" in the New England sense of the phrase?

Some persons, probably, would solve the difficulty very readily by replying, that I have never been converted; that I am not now, and have never been, a Christian. This solution occurred to my own mind, and led me to self-examination; and the conclusion at which I arrived was, that if this view of the case was correct, I knew neither what it was to be a Christian, nor how to become one, and I saw no means of ever knowing. I certainly desired to know and believe the truth, and did receive as true the doctrines of the Bible so far as I could ascertain them; I certainly wished to know the will of God, however far I might be from being always willing to do it; and that he would leave me to perish through absolute inability to discover what he would have me do, I did not believe. I was, therefore, seldom troubled with doubts in regard to my own conversion. I was conscious of being a great sinner in the sight of God ; but I knew that I should have to contend against my evil inclinations as long as I lived, and never expected to be free from them while my soul dwelt in this body. On the other hand, I knew that in my better frames of mind I did earnestly desire to avoid sin, and that I never yielded to it without afterward sorrowing on account of it and praying for forgiveness ; and I believed that such a state of mind is produced and kept in activity only by the influences of the Holy Spirit. I was satisfied, therefore, that the difficulty in deciding when I was converted could not be solved by replying, as some might reply, "Never." It must remain an open question which I was unable to answer.

Thus far I have been describing my feelings and opinions as they were at the time when I came to New York, after having spent a year in preaching at various places. It is very possible you have often wondered why I so suddenly renounced the ministry ; if so, you now have the explanation. I was conscious of an entire unfitness to act as a teacher of others in regard to matters which concerned their eternal welfare, while I was so ignorant myself. I also knew that I held opinions which would exclude me from almost all the pulpits in which I was invited to preach, if I should make them generally known. I therefore determined to decline all such invitations, and to let my clerical profession quietly drop. It was then that I commenced my school in B——, and to the few requests which were at first occasionally made, that I would supply the place of an absent minister, I replied that my school required all my attention, and that I needed Sunday for a day of rest. It was not long before every one seemed to forget that I had ever pretended to be a clergyman, and this was just what I wished. Now I am about to enter upon a new phase of my religious experience.

You know that, during the twelve years of my residence in B——, I continued to attend the P—— church, and that on coming to this city nearly three years ago, I became a regular attendant at St. J——'s Episcopal Church; and you probably supposed that I had made this change merely as a matter of taste, because I preferred the Episcopal to the Congregational service. This was one reason, certainly. I thought the congregation should take some part in the exercises; that they should go to confess their sins and to pray for forgiveness themselves; not to sit while the minister does it for them. I had also been so often offended by the prayers to which I had been compelled to listen, but in which it was impossible for me to join, that

I had become convinced it is far better to have a prescribed form, than to allow the clergyman to stand up in the pulpit, and, under the pretence of acting as the spokesman of his people, pray for things which many of them do not desire, and perhaps in language that shocks their sense of propriety and of the reverence due to Almighty God. I need not say that I do not intend to apply these remarks to the prayers of Dr. ——. There would be no justice in my doing so, as every one knows who has been in the habit of attending his church; but they are applicable to those of a very large number of Non-Episcopal Protestant ministers. These considerations alone would have been sufficient to lead me to the resolution, which I had made several years before leaving B——, that whenever anything should occur to sever my connection with him as my pastor, I would join the Episcopal Church.

But I had other reasons of far more importance for finally taking this step. My religious views were gradually undergoing such a change during these twelve years that, at length, I could not conscientiously profess to believe in accordance with the "Articles of Faith" to which I was supposed to assent.

Of the boys who were members of my school,

about one half always were children of Episcopal parents, and many of the families in which I was most intimate were connected with that church. Hence I had an opportunity of comparing the effects upon young children of the different kinds of religious instruction to which they were subjected. On the one hand were those who had been brought up as outside the fold of Christ, totally depraved, wholly inclined to evil, and in need of constant watching to prevent their breaking away from all restraint; expected to do wrong rather than right, and not credited with right feelings toward any one, and least of all toward God, whom their sinful hearts must necessarily regard with hatred, because they were still in their natural state, not yet converted, though their parents hoped they would be in God's good time. I found that many of these boys were just what they were expected to be; false, deceitful, difficult of control by any appeal to their consciences or their sense of right, and apt to grow worse as they grew older.

On the other hand were those who had been brought up by their parents as lambs of Christ's flock; taught to regard themselves as young members of the church, made so by their baptism; expected to do voluntarily what they knew to be right; never told that all their most innocent actions were sinful and displeasing to a holy God, but, on the contrary, that God was their heavenly Father, who loved them and was pleased with them when they did right; taught that they should try to act as Christians from the very earliest age, so that they might be fitted for confirmation and to be admitted to the full privileges of the church as soon as they should be old enough. These boys, I found, were generally just what they were expected to be, truthful, reliable, amiable, and under the control of right moral feelings. The inference was irresistible: this teaching is true and right; the other is false and wrong.

I became satisfied, also, from my intercourse with members of the Episcopal communion, that those who had thus grown up into the church, without having gone through the prescribed course of conviction and conversion, which I had been taught to consider so essential, gave as good evidence in their lives of true piety, as could be found among the members of any other church. They could remember no period when they were not governed, to some extent at least, by religious principle; they had been confirmed while yet children, had been admitted at once to communion, and had lived consistent Christian lives ever since, without having thought of asking themselves, *when* they were converted, *when* they became Christians; and if such a question had been proposed to them, they would have replied that they were always Christians.

I was convinced they were right, and that nothing but the religious teaching to which they are subjected renders necessary, in the case of children of pious parents in other denominations, the violent change through which, at some time in their lives, they are expected to pass, under the name of conversion. They have been taught to consider themselves wholly given over to do evil; invited to look on when their parents engage in religious exercises, but excluded from all participation in them; told so constantly they are incapable of any right emotions, that they are careful not to manifest any lest they should be accused of hypocrisy; then, when a revival happens, they are worked up into a feverish state of excitement, trying to get themselves into such a frame of mind that God may be induced to "give them a new heart"—an operation of the nature of which they have not the slightest idea—and ready to seize upon any unusual feeling of mind or body in evidence that it is done. The change with them, if happily it come, is really a great one. Before, they were children of the devil, now, they are the chosen lambs of the flock. Before, every act of their lives, it matters not how pure may have been the motives that produced it, was steeped in sin and deserving of eternal punishment; now, every act is supposed to be acceptable to God, who will graciously pardon all the shortcomings of his beloved child. Before, they were watched, distrusted, disbelieved, suspected of vices which they hated, and accused of offences which they never thought of; now, they are received into favor, loved, caressed, rejoiced over, trusted in everything, suspected of nothing. It is, indeed, a mighty change to them, and there can be no wonder that they look back upon it to the end of their lives, as the turning-point at which they were snatched from the path which was leading them to destruction, and set down in the way to eternal life. But the necessity for this violent change has come from the nature of the doctrines held by their parents and taught to them, and from nothing else.

I once saw in the *Missionary Herald* an account of a revival among the children of the mission school at Ouroomiah, written by one of the missionaries, in which he describes the phenomena as being identical with those observed in similar cases in a New England village; whence he draws the inference that this is evidently the way, and the only way, in which the Holy Spirit operates, the world over, in converting sinners to righteousness. But his facts prove no such thing; they merely furnish an illustration of the familiar truth, that like causes produce like effects.

You must not suppose from what I have said that I intended to deny (for I am speaking of opinions held by me for years before I came here) either the reality of the change which occurs in conversion, or the agency of the Holy Spirit in producing it. Its reality was evident from the fact, that men who before had lived in the practice of open sin, and who had mocked at all religious principle, did now manifestly reform their lives and endeavor to conform their conduct to the precepts of the Bible; from being bad men, they did become good men. This was a fact patent to the observation of every one, and I believed that all such reformations are wrought through the influence of God's spirit working upon the soul. But on the other hand, I believed that the degree of such change is very various, depending entirely upon the previous character. In those who have always lived in persistent rebellion against what they knew to be their duty, and who have given unchecked sway to their evil inclinations, the change must necessarily be deep and violent; on the other hand, in young persons, examples of whom may be found in abundance in Christian families, who seem always to have been under the influence of right moral feelings, and who have never been happy with the consciousness of having done wrong until they have confessed their fault and been forgiven, the change is a very slight one, except just so far as it is made important by the opinions of their parents and religious teachers; and if they were brought up under a right system of instruction, it would be either wholly unnecessary, or would take place so quietly and at so early an age, that the subject of it might know nothing about it. Between these two extremes, there would naturally be every intermediate degree of change in the affections and the life.

The result of my observations and reflections was a conviction that there is no necessity that all persons should pass through the peculiar experiences called in New England "conviction" and "conversion," and that the children of the church, if properly educated, might be expected to grow up into mature Christians as naturally as the kernel of wheat grows into a wheat-stalk and not into a thistle.

This conviction necessarily led to a change in my opinions in regard to "regeneration." Hitherto I had never thought of it as being anything else than the "conversion" of Calvinists. But having become convinced that this may, in many cases, be of very little practical importance, if not absolutely unnecessary, I was obliged to seek elsewhere for the "new birth," which it is evident, from the stress laid upon it by our Lord, cannot be regarded in so trivial a light. His words are very explicit: "Except a man be born again, he cannot see the kingdom of God." If, therefore, this new birth does not take place in conversion, where are we to look for it? The answer seemed to me a very plain one; so plain that I wondered I had never seen it before. It is contained in the reply of our Saviour to the wondering question of Nicodemus: "Except a man be born *of water* and of the Spirit, he cannot enter into the kingdom of God." Christians of the sect to which I belonged wholly ignore the words "of water" in this text. That they refer to the water of baptism no one denies; they can by no possibility mean anything else. Yet these Christians, while believing that a man must be born of the Spirit, deny that he must be or is born of water. This is evident from the fact that they refuse baptism to an unbaptized adult, unless they have what they consider satisfactory evidence that he has already been regenerated in conversion. He must have been "born again" before being baptized, or they will not baptize him; hence, if he is born of water at all, it must be a second new birth, supplemental to the former. These persons hold no such opinion as this; they reject altogether the doctrine that regeneration takes place in baptism; yet the fact is declared in this text, in language as clear and unequivocal as are the words which can be adduced in proof of any article of Christian faith. They must mean this or have no meaning at all.

But decisive as is this text, there is other evidence in abundance that regeneration takes place in baptism. The rite, as practised in Calvinistic churches, means nothing and effects nothing, so far as the recipients are concerned, when applied to young children. Hence, if a child should die unbaptized, it is considered of no consequence whatever. But such views are entirely inconsistent with the importance evidently attached to the rite in the New Testament. It is unnecessary for me to refer to particular texts in proof of this; you need only read the Bible yourself, with this thought in your mind, in order to be convinced of it.

Finally, I was satisfied that it had always, from the earliest ages, been the doctrine of the church, that baptism is something more than a mere dedication of the child to God on the part of its parents. All history shows this, and the language of the Nicene Creed, which few deny was the creed of the church long before the "corruptions of popery" were introduced, proves it: "I acknowledge one baptism for the remission of sins."

Some objections to this view of regeneration presented themselves to my mind, but all seemed to admit of reasonable answers. In the first place, if the new birth occurs in baptism, many persons are regenerated who are never converted to righteousness. It appeared to me that two replies could be made to this, either of which might be the true one. It is evident from the term used to designate it that regeneration is purely an act of God in which the subject of it is as passive as in his natural birth. What is the nature of the change produced I did not profess to know, but had no doubt that it freed the individual from some evil inherent in human nature as a consequence of the sin of our first parents, and I saw no necessary connection between this act of divine power and mercy and the subsequent turning from the world to God, which is the act of the sinner himself. Or, if this reply is unsatisfactory, we may suppose, I argued, that God, who knows in every individual case whether the recipient of baptism will be a true Christian in after life or not, makes the regenerative power of the rite dependent upon what he knows will be the future action of the baptized person.

Again, supposing this doctrine of baptismal regeneration to be true, many persons are converted before being regenerated. I saw no difficulty in this. It is the duty of all men to love and serve God whether regenerate or not, and whatever man ought to do, he can do; for it has always seemed to me a self-evident proposition that where there is no ability there is no obligation. If, therefore, an unregenerate man can repent and turn to God, there is no reason for denying that, under the influence of the Holy Spirit, he sometimes does.

Again, a person may be truly converted and suddenly die before being baptized: how can he enter the kingdom of heaven? My reply to this was, God holds the lives of all men in his hands, and if he takes from any one the power of complying with his requirements, he will undoubtedly accept the will for the deed.

You will understand that no one but myself is responsible for the views which I have been expressing; I am stating merely the operations of my own mind in relation to these questions. I had never read the writings of any advocate of the doctrine of baptismal regeneration, and do not know at the present time whether they would answer the above objections as I have done. I only know that these answers seemed satisfactory to me.

This view of regeneration solved the difficulty in

deciding the time of my own conversion. I believed that I had been "born again" in the water of baptism, and conversion being nothing more than a turning of the affections from the world to God, I saw no reason why it might not occur more than once. Indeed, every act of penitence is a partial conversion toward God, as every sinful act is a partial retroversion from him.

Holding these views in regard to the effect and importance of baptism, it is evident that I could not consistently continue my connection with a church, one of the articles of whose creed is, that "only believers (by which word is meant, members of the church) and their infant children are proper subjects of Christian baptism." If my ideas were correct, it would be horribly wrong to refuse baptism to any one, or to the children of any one, who might be willing to receive it for them or himself, even though he should refuse to perform any other Christian duty. Our Saviour's command is: "Go ye, therefore, and teach all nations, baptizing them;" yet here was a church professing to do the former in obedience to the command, and positively refusing to do the latter except to those who would subscribe to certain dogmas which it did not itself dare to say were essential to salvation. Far better would it be to do as Protestant historians say was done in former days by Catholic missionaries—seize upon all persons who fell into their hands, and baptize them even against their will.

I have brought my narrative down to the time of my coming to W——, nearly three years ago, and you now see the motives which led me to connect myself with the Episcopal Church. In the first place, I preferred a form of service in which I could feel that I was myself taking a more important part than that of a listener; secondly and chiefly, the church has a creed to which I could give my assent.

But in enrolling myself as a member of this church, did I intend to acknowledge her right to prescribe to me authoritatively what I should believe? Certainly not. "The Bible alone" was still my rule of faith as much as before, and I considered myself under no more obligation to receive the Thirty-nine Articles as of divine authority, than the "Confession of Faith" of any New England congregation. Both are alike the expression of merely human opinions; both alike are to be received or rejected according as they do or do not seem to me to be sustained by the word of God. The creeds, those called the "Apostles'" and the "Nicene," I accepted without questioning, and supposed that I did so because I was convinced they are thus sustained; at least, I should undoubtedly have given this as my reason if asked why I believed them.

But I soon discovered that I had an entirely different reason for receiving them and rejecting the authority of the "Articles of Religion." This was, that I knew the creeds were almost as old as the Christian religion, and expressed the faith of the church as it had been from the earliest ages, while the "articles" date back no further than the reigns of Edward the Sixth and Elizabeth. It may appear strange that it did not at once occur to me, that in this I had abandoned my rule of faith—the Bible alone—and had adopted another, namely, the teachings of the early church. But I did not think of this until some time afterward; for the moment I stepped outside of the creeds, I saw no means of ascertaining what these teachings were. Anterior to the "Reformation" there was but one church, and whatever we now possess which is true has been handed down through successive ages by her. But I had always believed that this truth has been so buried under errors and corruptions, that it is now almost impossible to dig it out from under the mass of rubbish in which it is concealed. The creeds stand out clear and distinct above it, firm and immovable as the primitive rock, and upon them I felt secure; but all around them I saw nothing on which I could venture to trust my foot. In taking the teachings of the early church, therefore, for my rule of faith, and having to depend upon my own sagacity in discovering what they were, I should have been far worse off than with the "Bible alone."

And now, for the first time in my life, I began to suspect that the opinions in which I had been educated, and the truth of which I had never questioned, in regard to the Catholic Church, were not quite correct. Two years ago, M—— began sending me *The Catholic World*, and I read the successive numbers as they appeared, merely from curiosity, to see how the advocates of this absurd superstition would attempt to defend it in the brilliant light of this nineteenth century. But I soon found, to my astonishment, that the sentiments expressed by the writers who supplied the pages of the magazine were wholly irreconcilable with what I had always supposed to be the doctrines of the church. The discovery was so unexpected that I was absolutely bewildered by it, and was in the condition of the seaman who should suddenly find all his old landmarks, which he had considered as firm as the earth itself, beginning to shift and dance about, and disappear, at last, altogether. I no longer knew what to depend upon, or whether I could depend upon anything. Had the church changed her doctrines? This I knew she certainly had not done since the Council of Trent, in the sixteenth century; yet I had never doubted that she held doctrines which evidently were not held by the writers or the conductors of this magazine, which is endorsed by the highest authorities of the church as an exponent of Catholic opinions.

The first thing which began to open my eyes was finding the massacre of Bartholomew's incidentally spoken of in a manner quite like to that in which I had been used to speak of it myself. I had been taught that this slaughter was instigated by the pope, that it was and is justified and defended by all Catholics, and that at the time of its occurrence it was made the subject of a special *Te Deum* at Rome. This I found to be assumed as all false; its falsity not spoken of as a matter which was to be argued, but taken for granted in such a way as to show that the writer supposed all his readers knew it to be false. I had regarded it as a doctrine of the church that heretics were to be extirpated without mercy by fire and sword; and I found religious persecution condemned as strongly as it could be by any Protestant review. I had believed it to be a doctrine of the church, that "the end sanctifies the means," and that it is right to do evil that good may come;" and I found such doctrines never alluded to except with abhorrence. I had been taught that the priests professed to pardon sin by their own power; that they sold pardons for money, and sold even permissions to commit sin, pardoning it in advance before it was committed. I found that the contributors to *The Catholic World* knew nothing of such doctrines. I had been taught that the Catholic religion is one of merely exterior forms and ceremonies, having very little of inward piety; yet I found all the articles of this periodical pervaded with a spirit of piety apparently more genuine, more fervent, and more uniformly consistent than I had ever seen in other writings even professing to be "religious." The writers seemed not to have put on their religion for some special purpose, intending to take it off like a holiday dress when the occasion should be over, but they wore it always and everywhere, as their ordinary working-day raiment. Laying down *Harper's* or *The Atlantic* and taking up *The Catholic World* seemed like going from a pagan temple into a Christian church; and I found myself becoming a better Christian, from month to month, through the influence of this oracle of a "corrupt church," learning to love God and my fellowmen more and more, day by day, through the teachings of those who, if my old instructors were to be believed, have no such love themselves. A most marvellous result truly!

Then turning my attention from these writings to the living representatives of the Catholic faith whom I saw everywhere around me, whose whole lives are spent in doing good, and who are looking for no reward in this world for their self-sacrificing charity, the conclusion which I could not avoid was: Protestants may talk as much as they please about the "corruptions" of the Catholic Church; but if, as our Lord said, a tree is to be known by its fruits, there can be nothing very corrupt about this old church as it exists among us, whatever it may have been in the days of Martin Luther. That it is now and here a true church of Christ, I have not a shadow of doubt.

Having made this acknowledgment, it was plainly impossible for me to stop here. This church claims to be, not merely *a* church, but *the* church; she claims to speak by divine authority, and demands obedience from all Christians. It is evident that, if she has this authority, she supplies just what I have felt the need of all my life—a reliable interpreter of the word of God. At length I began to think her claims might be well founded, and by a gradual process of change my admission of the possibility of this was converted, through the operations of my own mind, into a conviction of its probability, and finally into a full belief in its truth. Throughout this process, which was going on during a period of nearly a year, I went to no Catholic, layman or priest, for advice or instruction, and I read no Catholic books, being resolved, that in case I should eventually become a convert to their faith, you and my friends should be unable to say I had been led astray by the craft and deceit of priests and Jesuits. It was not until nothing remained as an obstacle in the way of my going to what I believed to be the only true church of Christ, except some of the charges made against her by Protestants, which I had never seen answered though I had no doubt they had been, that I sought an interview with a Catholic priest. He gave me to read *Milner's End of Controversy*. If this book had been written expressly to meet my wants, it could not have done it better. Before I had finished it my hesitation was at an end, my resolution was made, and now I thank my God, morning and evening and all day long, that he has so mercifully opened my eyes to see the truth to which for so many years I have been blind. My doubts and difficulties are over; I know what the Bible requires me to believe and do, because I have found the Philip whom I needed as an interpreter of the sacred writings, but whom I have longed for in vain all my life, not suspecting he was so near me.

As I have kept no record of the successive steps by which, during the last two years, I have been advancing toward my present position, I cannot state them in chronological order. I can only give you the general results, with the considerations which have led to them, and in doing so I shall be obliged to repeat to some extent what I have already said. I will endeavor, however, to avoid this as far as possible. I hope you will reflect upon each of these considerations which appear to me so convincing, and, if you think any of my premises false or my deductions erroneous, that you will point them out to me, in order that I may see them as you do, provided your view of them is most in accordance with truth; for to know the truth is undoubtedly the desire equally of both of us. Remember, also, that it is illogical and irrational to deny the conclusion, while you are unable to show where the reasoning which leads to it is false, unless you have such evidence of its falsity as ought to be satisfactory to every one who means to believe what God has said, whether it is sustained by argument or not. If you have any such evidence of the falseness of the religion taught by the Catholic

Church, I should be able to see it as well as yourself, and it would be wrong in you to withhold it from me.

The first conclusion at which I arrived as the result of my reflections was this: The Bible alone is not a sufficient rule of faith; by which I mean that it is not such a guide to God's truth that all men, or indeed that any man, merely from a study of its pages, can ascertain with absolute assurance what are its teachings, or can be certain that his opinions, when formed, may not possibly be erroneous.

At the risk of giving my narrative the appearance of a doctrinal treatise, I will, for the sake of distinctness, mark with figures and letters the steps of the reasoning which has led me to this conclusion.

(1.) My own experience has shown me that, however sufficient the Bible alone may be for other men, it is quite insufficient for me. The foregoing history of my past spiritual life must convince you also of this fact.

(2.) There is internal evidence in the Bible itself that it cannot be a sufficient rule of faith.

(*a.*) The truths of the Christian religion are not there stated clearly and distinctly, so that even the unlearned man, by a mere perusal of the book, can understand what it intends to teach; and it is impossible to reconcile this obscurity with the doctrine that every man is required to learn the truth from it alone, and will be punished for ever if he fails to do so. So evident is this that Protestants are forced to admit it; and, in order to avoid the necessary consequence, they have to fall back upon the assertion that God will himself explain his word to those who ask him to do so. This would be satisfactory, were it not that, if the assurances of pious, devout men of various faiths are worth anything, God has, under just these circumstances, given as many different explanations of his teachings as there are different creeds in the world, and those who hold the most contradictory opinions are alike confident that they have been enlightened from on high.

(*b.*) It is evident that the sacred writers themselves had no suspicion that their writings would, in future ages, be regarded as containing the whole code of the Christian religion. The gospels are mere narratives of some of the events which occurred in the life of our Lord, and are designed to be nothing more; even as such they are, according to the testimony of St. John, very incomplete. Most of the Epistles of St. Paul were written for purely local purposes, and allude to points of doctrine only so far as these have a bearing upon the special object which he had in view. He also constantly assumes that his readers are familiar with circumstances which gave rise to his letters, and a knowledge of which is essential to their proper understanding, but of which we know little or nothing. He also makes allusion to customs and doctrines in so cursory a manner that we can form no definite idea of his meaning, at the same time promising to explain by word of mouth those things which may not be understood by his readers. It appears to me that no one can read his epistles with the object kept before the mind, of judging whether, in writing them, he had any other than a local and temporary end in view, without being convinced that, if he had, it is not apparent.

(*c.*) We have the testimony of St. Peter that there are in the Epistles of St. Paul "some things nard to be understood, which they that are unlearned and unstable wrest, as also the other Scriptures, unto their own perdition." He does not say, they who are perverse and wilfully blind, but they that are "unlearned and unstable," that is, not established, fixed in their faith. Now, if knowledge of and stability in the truth are to be acquired only from a study of the Scriptures, every man must be both unlearned and unstable when he first enters upon that study. The words of the apostle, therefore, must mean one or the other of two things: either, that there are some things in the Epistles of St. Paul which any man, who, with a consciousness of his own ignorance, searches them for instruction, may misunderstand and thereby destroy himself, and that this is also true of the other Scriptures; or, that before venturing upon an examination of the Scriptures for himself, he should, by some other means, have acquired such a knowledge of the truth and such stability of faith as to render him secure against the danger of misinterpretation. Whichever of these two explanations you may choose to adopt, both are equally fatal to the Protestant dogma, that "the Bible alone is a sufficient Rule of Faith."

(3.) This doctrine is not really held by Protestants themselves.

(*a.*) This is proved by their practice. I need not dwell upon this point, having done so sufficiently already. Every one must admit it who reflects, that Protestants are careful to teach their children what they themselves regard as truth, long before those children are old enough to understand the Bible; and if the child, on becoming a man, should, through a study of the Scriptures, abandon the faith of his parents and adopt another adverse to theirs, he is condemned and excommucated as a rebel. He may make the Bible his rule of faith as long as he consents to interpret it as his religious teachers have done, but no longer. I will venture an assertion which you will probably regard as extravagant, but which, nevertheless, I believe to be strictly true. It is this: that most Christian parents would refrain from urging upon their children the reading of the Bible—that very many of them would endeavor to prevent it—if they supposed the result of such reading would be, the rejection by a child of the doctrines held by themselves and his adoption of those of some rival sect. But they know from experience and observation that the danger of this result is so exceedingly small that they need feel no anxiety in regard to it.

(*b.*) Protestants admit that it is hazardous for a man to enter upon the study of the Bible with the assumption that he knows nothing already of Scripture doctrine, and that everything is to be learned from the written word. This is a very singular admission when coupled with the assertion that he must derive his faith from those Scriptures and from them alone. He must study the Bible in order to ascertain what he is required to believe; but he should first be careful to have decided what he will believe, or else it is possible, it is even probable, that he will fall into dangerous errors. The inconsistency of these two doctrines is so manifest, when they are thus placed side by side, as to be positively ludicrous ; yet they are both held by the great mass of pious Protestants, in total unconsciousness of their incompatibility. What should we think of a professor of law, who begins his course of lectures to a class of students by telling them, they should not enter upon their legal studies with the assumption that they have learned nothing of law already, and that everything is to be learned from their books and teachers, for in so doing they would be likely to adopt very erroneous notions? What would be thought of a professor of medicine, who commences his instructions by warning his pupils against the danger of studying the nature and treatment of diseases without having first formed their own opinions in regard to these matters? Yet I well remember that, in opening his course of lectures upon theology when I was a student, the professor warned his class against starting from the position, that no religious truth is already known by them, and that everything is to be learned as they advance ; saying that he had known several instances in which students had done so with the most honest intentions, expecting one doctrine to be proved after another. just as one demonstration follows another in geometry; but the result was, that they left the seminary as infidels. In reflecting upon this statement, I was convinced that his words of caution were wise, and might be necessary to some persons; for I was conscious that I admitted the truth of the doctrines held by myself, not because I was sure they could be proved from the Bible, but simply because, after my long period of scepticism, I felt the necessity of having some religious creed, and had resolved by a mere act of the will to believe what seemed most likely to be the truth.

(*c.*) Protestants hold as revealed truth what is not taught at all in the Bible.

Here you will probably open your eyes in amazement, wondering what I can mean; but I think you will be compelled to acknowledge, after having read what I am about to write, that you do yourself believe now, and have always believed, as of divine authority, doctrines which have not a shadow of support in the Scriptures.

You admit that the Decalogue is a universal law, designed for all men and all times, not abrogated, as was the Jewish ceremonial law, by the coming of Christ, and that you are now required to obey that law just as much as if no Messiah had ever appeared. Now read your Fourth Commandment and tell me whether you are obeying it; whether you ever obeyed it in your life: "The seventh day is the Sabbath of the Lord thy God: in it thou shalt do no work." You have set aside a plain command of that terrible law, given by Jehovah amid the lightnings and thunders of Sinai, a law written with his own finger upon the tables of stone; and you certainly would not dare to do this, unless you have evidence the most conclusive, evidence which cannot be questioned, that God has himself consented to its abrogation. Search your Bible for this evidence, and what do you find? Nothing except the statement, in Acts xx. 7, that on a certain occasion the disciples came together on the first day of the week to break bread, and that Paul preached to them. You certainly cannot regard the record of this event, which may have been, for aught which you know to the contrary, an extraordinary meeting, caused by the intended departure of the apostle on the morrow, as furnishing a sufficient ground for habitually disobeying one of the commands of the Decalogue. The first day of the week is nowhere called the Sabbath; this name is always used to designate the seventh, and you admit that you are bound to observe the Sabbath as much as were the Israelites, except that you have taken the liberty of changing it from the dav appointed by God himself to another day appointed by nobody, so far as can be ascertained from Scripture.

In order to show the force of this argument, let us suppose that Christians in all parts of the world had always, down to the present day, observed the seventh day of the week as the Sabbath, in accordance with the law of Mount Sinai, and that now, for the first time in the world's history, some self-styled reformer should endeavor to persuade them that their Lord intended to change the Sabbath from the seventh to the first day, and, when asked to furnish his evidence of this, should refer to the above text in the Acts of the Apostles, and to that in the Revelation of St. John, which shows that some day was known to the Christians of his time as the "Lord's day," though whether it was a particular day of the week, or of the month, or of the year, we have no means of deciding. Suppose, on no better evidence than this, he should attempt to change the practice of the church, how much success do you think he would have? Would not his reasoning be met with a universal laugh of contempt? Would he not be regarded as a crazy fanatic, unworthy of a serious answer? Yet this argument would be just as sound then, when urged in support of a proposed change, as it is now, when offered in explanation of a change actually existing.

If it would be ridiculous in the former case, it is equally ridiculous in the latter. Have I, then, or have I not, proved my point, that in believing the first day of the week is to be observed as the Sabbath, your faith is not founded on the Bible?

Again, the same admission must be made in regard to your belief in the validity of infant baptism. Not a syllable in support of the doctrine can be found in the Bible; and this is so palpably true, that theologians of the very sects which insist most strongly upon trying all doctrines by Scripture alone, are obliged to abandon their principle so far as this is concerned, and to acknowledge that it rests wholly upon the practice of the church in all ages. When fairly driven to the wall, they bring forward the absurd argument, that in two or three instances persons are said to have been baptized with their households, and the probability is that there were infants in some of these families; and as the sacred writers do not say that these infants (supposing that there were any) were not baptized, it follows, of course, that they were. This is just about as logical as it would be for you to infer, from my saying that Mr. A. and Mr. B. and Mr. C., with their families, partook of the sacrament, last Sunday, that it is customary in W—— to give the sacramental bread and wine to infants; for the probability is that there is at least one infant in these three families, and, as I have not said these infants did not receive the sacrament, I must be understood as implying that they did. The persons to whom, or for whom, the apostles wrote, knew whether it was customary to baptize infants, as well as you know whether it is usual to take them to communion; and if they were excluded from the former rite, it was no more necessary for the sacred penman to say so in order to avoid being misunderstood, than it would be for me to qualify my statement in the same way in my supposed letter to you.

The weakness of this argument from Scripture in support of infant baptism may be shown by trying it by the same test which I just now applied to that in defence of the Christian Sabbath. Suppose that, down to the present day, baptism had been confined to adults; and that now, for the first time, same one should propose to extend the rite to infants, urging the texts to which I have referred in evidence that such persons were baptized by the apostles; how many proselytes do you think he would obtain? You, and every person of ordinary intelligence, would reply: "Prove to us, first, that there were any infants in the household of Stephanus, and then prove that the Corinthian Christians were so ignorant that St. Paul, in order to avoid being misunderstood, would consider it necessary to tell them whether he was, or was not, in the habit of baptizing such persons—prove to us these two things, first, and then we may think what you say worthy of serious consideration ; but not till then."

What I have said with regard to the practice of infant baptism applies with equal force to that of baptism by sprinkling. In every instance in which the rite is so spoken of that we can form an opinion as to the manner in which it was performed, we know positively that it was not by sprinkling. Yet you believe such baptism to be valid without a particle of Scripture evidence in favor of your opinion. Have I not, then, proved my proposition, that Protestants believe things as articles of religious faith which are not taught in the Bible at all?

(*d.*) Protestants reject doctrines which are plainly taught in Scripture.

This proposition will be received by you with still more incredulity than the preceding, and you will suppose I am about to refer to what you would call the popish doctrines of auricular confession, purgatory, extreme unction, and other such things. But though all these can be better supported from the Bible than some of those which you profess to believe on Scripture authority, yet I need not allude to them at all in order to prove my position. There is one religious duty taught so plainly in the Bible that I do not see how any Christian can deny it; yet it is denied by almost all Protestant sects. I refer to the practice of fasting. The Episcopal Church has appointed her days of fasting, but leaves the observance of them wholly to the private judgment of her members, and few pay any regard to them. Christians of other denominations seldom even pretend to fast. Their argument is, that there can be nothing pleasing to God in a man's going without his dinner, and that the practice is a superstitious one. But that any person can read the New Testament, and see how constantly prayer and fasting are spoken of together as equally important and equally efficacious as means of grace, and then reject the one without at the same time renouncing the other, is marvellous. There is no need of my quoting texts to you in order to prove what I say; they are perfectly familiar to you now; and I am confident that, if you reflect upon this question with the Bible open before you, you must admit that there is no duty more plainly taught by our Lord than that of fasting. Yet you will confess that you have never fulfilled this duty any further than perhaps to make a light dinner once a year at the appointment of the civil government, and of late years very few Christians do even this. I acknowledge that I have never myself been in the habit of observing these annual fast-days, because I have never recognized the right of the governor of the state to prescribe to me my religious duties. At the same time, I have never doubted that our Lord did expect his disciples to fast after he should be taken from them as much as he expected them to pray; and as it is evident the Christians of the first ages so understood his commands, and practised in accordance with this understanding of them, it has always been a mystery to me why modern Christians should consider themselves relieved from this duty, and should have come to regard it as not only useless, but childish and semi-heathenish.

In denying, therefore, the necessity of fasting, Protestants deny what is plainly taught in the Bible.

To this I may add, so far as non-Episcopal sects are concerned, the rejection of the doctrine of regeneration by baptism, of which I have spoken already. If our Lord did not refer to regeneration when he said, "Except a man be born again, he cannot see the kingdom of God;" and if he did not refer to the water of baptism when he said, "Except a man be born of water and of the Spirit," then this doctrine may be false. On any other supposition, I see not how it can be. Yet I do not doubt that, if I should read this text to you on Monday, and ask whether the words "born again" denote regeneration, you would reply, "Yes, certainly;" if another person should read the same text on Tuesday, and ask you what the words "of water" mean, you would say, "Baptism, of course;" and if a third should ask on Wednesday whether you believe regeneration takes place in baptism, you would reply, with some wonder at the question, "No, certainly not." Try the experiment on some of your church members, and see if the result is not just what I have said.

(4.) The doctrine, that the Bible alone is a sufficient rule of faith, has given rise to hundreds of sects, which must, in the very nature of things, go on multiplying, so long as there is no recognized authority to which disputes may be referred. This division began when the authority of the church was first set aside, in violent and bitter quarrels between the leaders of the so-called "Reformation," Luther, and Calvin, and Zwingle, and it has continued and been fruitful in the propagation of new divisions ever since; and that it will still continue to be so is as certain as it is that what are now the terminal twigs of a tree will, if it continue to grow, branch into two or three new shoots, themselves to become stems for other branches. That this is an evil few persons calling themselves Christians can deny, and just at this time attempts are making in some quarters to remedy it. The leaders of the Old and New Schools of the Presbyterian Church are endeavoring to unite these two sects. They will probably fail; but even if they seem to succeed, the general result will amount to nothing. It is much as if a gardener should imagine that, by grafting together two terminal branches of a tree, he is beginning a process by which the whole tree-top may ultimately be reduced to a single trunk. He may possibly, by careful nursing, induce two twigs to grow into one; but the operation is contrary to nature, and they will immediately begin to divide again. So it is, and so it always must be, with religious sects, as long as every man has an indisputable right to form his own opinions in regard to the teachings of the Bible, and to persuade as many persons as he can to adopt them. If a man wishes to be at the head of something, and can draw a crowd after himself in no other way, he can generally do it by striking out some new system of religious faith.

(5.) This doctrine has led vast numbers of persons to the conclusion that, since there are very few articles of the Christian creed which can be established with certainty, it is of no importance what a man believes, so long as he is sincere, and acts according to his own convictions of duty. I have shown, in a former part of these pages, that this conclusion seems to be logically deduced from premises which cannot be disputed, and that I was myself greatly perplexed at seeing no means of escape from it, though I knew it could not be true.

(6.) The doctrine is absurd ; for it cannot be proved from the Bible, and must, therefore, be condemned when tried by the standard set up by itself. That all which the Bible teaches is to be received as God's truth, no one disputes ; but that the Bible anywhere teaches that its own pages contain *everything* which men ought to know and do, no one who has any regard for his own reputation would dare say to an intelligent audience. He would be required to produce chapter and verse, and this he would be totally unable to do.

(7.) The doctrine is absurd, because it is impossible to ascertain from the Bible what writings constitute the Bible. Protestants are so in the habit of thinking and speaking of the New Testament as a complete whole, that one would suppose, from their manner of expressing themselves, that the Gospels and Apostolic Epistles were collected together by the writers themselves in their present form, and were so handed down by them to succeeding generations. But every person acquainted with history knows, that for three hundred years these writings existed as separate, detached manuscripts, and that there were mixed with them a large number of others which were thought by many learned men to be equally apostolic with those which now form the canon of the New Testament. These manuscripts were collected and carefully examined by the fathers of the church, and it is from them that Protestants have received their Bible. In one respect, if in no other, they recognize the authority of the Catholic Church; that is, in receiving as sacred scripture just what the church has declared to be such, and rejecting everything else.

There seems to me something positively ludicrous in the implicit faith which Protestants have in the correctness of writings which have been handed down, for fourteen hundred years, by successive copyists, all of whom were devoted adherents of the very church which, according to them, has been, throughout this whole period, introducing corruption after corruption into both the faith and the practice of its members. Every ancient copy of the New Testament scriptures, to which Protestant commentators now appeal for the settlement of disputes in regard to the text, was written by, and has been preserved by, the disciples of the men who have introduced all these corruptions; yet no one suspects them of having corrupted these writings. The reason is plain: as Protestants have rejected the authority of the church, they are compelled to defend the correctness of the Scriptures; otherwise, they would have no rule of faith whatever; and the church owes it to this necessity, and to nothing else, that she has never had this accusation made against her. None of the original gospels or epistles are in existence, and the oldest existing copies were made from preceding copies, and no one knows how many generations of such transcripts there were between the original manuscripts and the oldest now extant. No one, therefore, can know, with certainty, that we have a single epistle of St. Paul just as it came from his hand. It would certainly have been far easier to introduce corruptions into these manuscripts, which were almost exclusively in the hands of the clergy, than into the faith which was the common possession of the whole body of the people. Yet the church is accused of having done the most difficult of the two things, and is not suspected of having attempted the easiest.

I have already said that there is internal evidence in the Scriptures themselves that the sacred writers had no idea they were composing a "sole rule of faith" for all future ages. The same thing is proved by the fact that no care seems to have been taken in a single instance to preserve the original manuscript. If one of St. Paul's epistles, written or signed with his own hand, were now in existence, it would be guarded as carefully as were the original tables of the law by the Jews. So they would all have been preserved by the primitive church, if she had regarded them in the same light in which they are regarded by Protestants now; and if the apostle had so viewed them, he would undoubtedly have given directions for their preservation. But they were probably worn out by frequent reading and handling, even before his death, leaving the care of perpetuating them in the hands of copyists, whom nothing but a miracle could secure against more or less mistakes; and that they did make mistakes in abundance, a comparison of ancient manuscripts sufficiently proves.

So much in justification of the first conclusion to which my examination led me; namely, that the Bible alone is not a sufficient rule of faith.

It is evident that, if I had stopped with an admission of the truth of the preceding proposition, I should have been like a ship in a fog, without chart or compass—unable to decide in what direction lay the rocks which I knew were somewhere about me, or what course I should steer in order to avoid them. I did not make this admission, therefore, until I was satisfied of the truth of the second proposition; which is, that our Lord established a body of living teachers, by whom he designed that his religion should be taught orally throughout all ages; and that the apostles, who were commissioned directly by himself, were only the first in a series which was intended to be perpetual, and which has continued down to the present day, and will continue to the end of the world.

The words addressed by our Saviour to the eleven before his ascension admit of no other interpretation: "Go, teach all nations," etc.: "teaching them to observe all things whatsoever I have commanded you: and, lo, I am with you alway," or, as it is in the Greek, "all days, even unto the end of the world." It is impossible to doubt that the promise in the last clause has reference to their proper fulfilment of the duty enjoined upon them in the preceding, they were to teach, and he would be with them to direct their teaching until—when?—the day of their death? No! but until the end of time.

I am almost ashamed to acknowledge that I have

been reading the Bible all my life, and have always put a wrong interpretation on this text. I have never attached any other meaning to the words, "the end of the world," than the furthest limits of the earth ; and, if I am not much mistaken, this idea is very commonly attached to them by Protestants. It comes naturally from associating this passage with the parallel one in St. Mark's Gospel: "Go ye into all the world," etc. The same English word being used in both places, those who can read the Bible in English only, will almost necessarily understand it in the same sense in both. I ought to have known better, for I had read the text in Greek often enough to have corrected the error, and my not having done so shows how persistently first impressions retain possession of the mind. I had heard these words quoted scores of times in evidence of the perpetuity of a teaching church, and had never recognized their force because of my wrong understanding of them. At length, on one such occasion, it suddenly occurred to me that they might not mean what I supposed ; and, on referring to the Greek, I found, to my surprise, that they could not have such a meaning ; that they signify "until the completion or termination of time," and can by no possibility signify anything else.

Now, to whom did our Lord give this commission

and this promise? To the eleven apostles only? If so, what did he mean by it? In what sense has he been with them as a guide in their teachings since their death? In what sense will he so be with them until the end of the world? The only intelligible explanation of the words is that which supposes there were to be, until the end of the world, living teachers, who should occupy the position then occupied by the eleven, having the same commission and the same authority; that they were to perpetuate their order by adding to their number, as circumstances might require. We know they began this process almost immediately, by enrolling Matthias among themselves, in the place of Judas, and there is no reason to doubt that they continued to do the same thing, at least as fast as vacancies occurred.

It may seem a very uncharitable thing to say, but I cannot avoid the suspicion that the translators of our English Bible knew they were obscuring this text by their version of it. The proper English equivalent of the preposition which they have rendered "unto," when followed, as in this case, by words denoting a future event, and, therefore, marking the limit of a period of time, is *until*, and so it is generally, if not always, translated in the New Testament. As I have no Greek concordance, I cannot say positively that this is the only passage in which, when so used, it is rendered "unto;" but I know of no other. Neither is it in accordance with present English usage to say that a thing shall continue "unto" the occurrence of some future event, nor was it, as I think, in accordance with usage in the days of James I. At all events, the meaning of the text would have been perfectly clear if the Greek word had received its ordinary translation of "until."

How this passage is explained by Protestant commentators, I have no means at hand of judging, as I have no commentary on the New Testament except that of Dr. Bloomfield, who says not a word in regard to it. As he must have known it to be one of the strong texts of the Catholic Church, I can only infer that he did not know how to explain it in harmony with Protestant ideas. He has a closely printed, double-columned, octavo page of comments on the eighteenth, nineteenth, and first half of the twentieth verses, but the last half of the last verse seems not to have been in his Bible.

In the second place, I believe in the perpetuity of an order of living teachers, because such teachers are absolutely necessary. They are necessary to individual Christians, who are in general unable to ascertain, from a study of the Bible alone, what they are required to believe and to do. If there are living men authorized to instruct them in these matters, as the apostles were authorized to teach the Christians of the first age, the whole difficulty in the case is removed at once. I need not dwell on this point, having spoken of it sufficiently already.

Such recognized teachers are also necessary to the church, as affording the only means by which the present divisions in the "body of Christ" can be healed. There should be unity in the church of Christ; this seems a self-evident proposition. Common sense tells us our Saviour never intended that those calling themselves his disciples should be divided and subdivided as they now are into numberless factions, holding different faiths, practising different baptisms, each party excluding all others from the Lord's table, and all contending quite as zealously against one another as against the wickedness which exists in the world. Parents and children, husbands and wives, brothers and sisters, all professing to be children of the same Heavenly Father, yet refusing to kneel before him at the same altar, to worship him in the same temple, to receive his sacraments from the same ministers. These things are shocking; yet they must continue until all are convinced that there is somewhere on the earth a body of teachers, who have authority from the Master himself to declare what he would have them believe and do. I am, and have long been, of the opinion that, if the leaders in the so-called "Reformation" of the sixteenth century could have anticipated the numerous divisions that would in future years spring out of their rejection of the authority of the church, they would have been filled with dismay at the prospect, and would have seen then, what is plainly to be seen now, that they should have been satisfied with endeavoring to bring about any needed reforms in the church itself, and not have gone deliberately to work to rend it to pieces. If by no other means than this could abuses be corrected, they should have left the matter to the disposal of the Lord of the church, waiting for him to order events in his own time and way, not daring to lift their sacrilegious hands against an organization which he had himself established, and which St. Paul declares to be the "body of Christ," he being the Head of that body. What kind of a body Protestants have made of it is apparent to every one ; each limb declaring itself to be the only one in union with the Head, and refusing to act in harmony with any other.

The testimony of the Bible to the necessity of oneness in the church is so abundant that page after page might be filled with quotations to that effect. "There shall be one fold and one shepherd." "That they may be one as we are;" a most remarkable text; as truly one as the Father and the Son are one! "Neither pray I for these alone, but for them also which shall believe on me through their word; that they all may be one." "That they may be made perfect in one;" that is, in unity, for the Greek word "one" in this passage is neuter, and does not mean one person. All these are the words of our Lord himself. The Epistles of St. Paul are full of exhortations to unity: "Endeavoring to keep the unity of the Spirit in the bond of peace. One body, and one Spirit; as ye are called in one hope of your calling. One Lord, one faith, one baptism." It would be a waste of time to go on quoting such texts, as you can find them in abundance on turning over the leaves of your New Testament; and the chief object of St. John in his First Epistle seems to have been to exhort Christians to love one another. Yet, in the face of the Bible and in defiance of common sense, some theologians are found who have the hardihood to justify the divisions in the church on the ground that they promote Christian zeal. They might as rationally argue that it would be a good thing for the right hand to be constantly acting in opposition to the left, because it would promote a development of the muscles.

In the third place, that there is a body of living teachers, speaking with divine authority, has always been believed in the Christian church, and until the " Reformation " was never denied by any body of men calling themselves Christians. I do not intend to produce evidence of this, as the burden of proof rests upon those who assert what I deny. I merely state it as a fact of which I have no doubt, and which I think no one can doubt who will candidly investigate the matter.

Finally, this is really the doctrine of the very sects which most stubbornly insist that they have received their faith from the Bible alone. The Lutherans condemn every departure from the dogmas of their founder, as if it were equivalent to a rejection of the revealed will of God. The followers of John Calvin used formerly to view in the same light every variation from his teachings ; but in later times so many have cut themselves loose from him, that different bodies have now very different authorities to which they appeal. The Presbyterians generally receive as authoritative the doctrines of the Westminster Assembly. The Congregationalists appeal, some to one and some to another noted theologian, living or dead, and require all their church members to receive his opinions as decisive. Those who know not where else to go conform their faith to the creed of their minister, judging that he ought to know better than they what is to be believed. He has been educated to teach them religion, just as their physician has been educated to heal their bodily diseases, and they trust their souls to the former with the same confidence with which they commit their bodies to the care of the latter. I have no doubt that ninety-nine out of every hundred persons professing to be Christians would admit without hesitation that they recognize some body as having authority to teach them religious truth, provided they were questioned in such a way as not to arouse a suspicion in their minds that the question was designed to entrap them into a confession that their faith is not founded on the Bible alone. It is practically the doctrine of all sects that Christians are to be taught orally, by living teachers ; and this is good Catholic doctrine, which has come down to them from the apostolic church, and which has lived through the three hundred and fifty years of separation from the only authorized living teacher, and which, in God's good time, will carry them back to her.

The doctrine, that religious truth is to be taught by the mouths of living men, is so consistent with reason, and supplies so exactly the want of which every one must be conscious who endeavors by his own efforts to ascertain what that truth is, that undoubtedly many persons have wished there were such teachers, divinely authorized to instruct them, and have wondered why there are none. On the other hand, it is so unreasonable, so apparently absurd, to expect the ignorant masses, the common people, whom our Lord declares he came expressly to teach, to learn this truth from the study of a book which very many of them cannot even read in their vernacular tongue, and the meaning of which cannot be agreed upon by the wise and learned—this expectation is so unreasonable that no sensible person would entertain it for a moment, if he were not absolutely compelled to do so. But, as I have said several times before, there is no escape from it when the authority of a teaching church is thrown aside.

This point being established to my entire satisfaction, that our Lord founded a church which was to endure throughout all time, and which, therefore, exists now, and one of the prerogatives of which is authority to teach all things whatsoever he has commanded, and whose teachings all men are required to receive, it only remained for me to find this church. It must, of course, be "visible," for an invisible church cannot be a teaching church. Whatever other attributes it may possess, it certainly cannot have this, and this is the very one of which I was in need.

Except the "Roman" Church, there is but one in this country that makes any pretence to speak with authority; this is, the Protestant Episcopal. Her claims were, therefore, the only ones which I was required to examine, and I did this with a perfect willingness to acknowledge their validity if I could discover it, and a hope that I might be able to do so; for I had no desire to take a step which would be viewed with indignation by some of my friends, and with contempt by others; a step which some would attribute to knavery, and others, by a stretch of charity, to nothing worse than foolishness. With one single exception, I had not a relative or friend to welcome me into the Roman Catholic Church; all were outside; almost all would, and all might, withdraw their confidence from me the moment they should learn that I had crossed its threshold.

But the very first question which I was called to consider in relation to the Episcopal Church was, Does she claim authority to teach the Gospel? Some of her ministers certainly claim it for her; but does she claim it for herself? I presume the rector of the church which I had been attending would endorse everything which, down to this very page, I have hitherto said, merely premising that the word "Protestant," wherever I have used it, does not include his church, and that the word "Catholic" does. He, and those who agree with him, who are commonly called "High-Church Episcopalians," maintain the divine right of their church to "teach all nations;" but, as I asked before, does the Episcopal Church claim it? If so, I do not know where. The Twentieth "Article of Religion" does, indeed, say, "The church hath authority in controversies of faith;" but the same article admits the possibility of her teaching error, and if she can do so, who is to decide whether she does or not? She has authority to teach so long as she teaches truth, but her authority ceases when she promulgates error. So has every other church this authority; so has Martin Luther, or Emanuel Swedenborg, or Joseph Smith, or any other man. The authority is vested in the truth which is taught, not in the persons who teach it. A church which can teach error has no authority at all in herself; the truth which she teaches must be received because it is truth, not because she teaches it, and, whether it is truth or not, every man must judge for himself.

This throws me back upon my own resources as much as if there were no such church.

But what is meant by "the church" in this Twentieth Article? As I have before said, a teaching church must be a visible church; probably no one will deny this; and the Nineteenth Article declares that "the visible church of Christ is a congregation of faithful men, in the which the pure word of God is preached, and the sacraments be duly ministered according to Christ's ordinance, in all those things that of necessity are requisite to the same." Is this the church which "hath authority in controversies of faith," and to which I am to apply for a solution of my doubts? If so, she would be of no use to me, even though she could speak with the authority of Gabriel, for I should never know whether I had found her. But this cannot be what is meant by "the church" in the Twentieth Article, for it would make as many churches, all having authority, as there are such congregations; and it is not probable that the compilers of the Book of Common Prayer intended to imply that there is only one such church, or even a small number of them. What, then, is meant by "the church" that hath authority?

I can find no definition of any such body in the Prayer-Book, but in the Creeds mention is made of a church to which the definition given in the Nineteenth Article will not apply, and this is undoubtedly the one referred to in the Twentieth. "I believe in the holy Catholic Church;" "I believe one Catholic and Apostolic Church." What church is this? Is it the Protestant Episcopal? In what sense is this church one? Almost as many varieties of doctrine are taught in it as by all other Protestant sects put together. The English and American churches, even, have not the same Creeds—the American Prayer-Book not containing the Athanasian, which is retained in the English. It is useless to argue this point. What I was in want of was, not a church in which I could quietly settle myself with all my own opinions left undisturbed, but a church which would decide for me the questions which I was unable to decide for myself, and whose decisions I could believe of divine authority. The want of unity in her teachings at different times, and even in different places at the same time, furnished most convincing evidence that this church has no such authority. I was also satisfied that neither the compilers of the English Book of Common Prayer, nor the American bishops who revised it for use in this country, ever thought of claiming for their church a right to teach religious truth with divine authority. This is altogether a recent idea, as is correctly maintained by the "Low Church' controversial writers.

In order that you may understand my objections to the Episcopal Church, it is necessary for you to keep distinctly in mind, that I had already decided that there is, somewhere on the earth, a church established, in a rudimentary form indeed, by Christ himself, and to which still belong, as truly as to the persons to whom they were first addressed, the command to preach the Gospel, and the promise that our Lord would guide them in so doing; and it is this church which I was seeking. The doctrines of the Episcopal Church might appear Scriptural, her worship might be pleasing; her clergy learned and sincere; her laity possessing every Christian virtue; all these things I might and did admit. But I required something more than all these; this was, such unity and such distinctness in her teachings as should afford satisfactory evidence that she speaks merely as the audible voice of God. But these are wholly wanting. Her own clergy hold opinions and preach doctrines as totally diverse as are those of any conflicting sects, and which of these are the doctrines of "the church" there is no authority to decide. If the true church is "one," she cannot be this church.

But she does not possess the other attributes of

the Nicene Creed any more than she possesses unity. She certainly makes no pretension to catholicity. The English Church is the "Church of England," and never pretended to be anything else; and the American never claimed to be anything more than an offshoot from the English, and cannot possess properties not possessed by that from which she has derived her existence.

Just as little can she claim to be apostolic, without at the same time either claiming to be one with the "Roman" Church, or admitting that there are two apostolic churches, teaching very different doctrines. She confesses necessarily that the "Church of Rome" was the apostolic church through all ages down to the time of her own separation from it; for it is from it that she professes to have derived her own apostolicity; and, so far as I know, no churchman pretends that, in imparting this quality to her, the Catholic Church lost it herself. "High-Church" writers endeavor to avoid this difficulty by calling their organization a "branch" of the Catholic, Apostolic Church. But if this is a branch, where is the trunk? If the Roman Church is that trunk, we have the anomaly of a dead tree bearing a living branch. If that church is herself only a branch, then again, I ask, where is the trunk? I see no answer to this question, except by falling back upon that "invisible church," to which we may attribute every possible invisible excellence, but which cannot have the practical quality of an ability to teach the ignorant. I have never heard repeated those words of the Nicene Creed, "I believe one Catholic, Apostolic Church," without wondering what idea is attached to them by the people around me, or whether they attach any meaning to them whatever. It appears to me now, that any intelligent Episcopalian, who will seriously ask himself the question, "What do these words mean which I am repeating almost every Sunday?" must come to the conclusion that he is declaring his belief in a different church from his own.

If, therefore, there now exist any church having authority to teach the religion of Jesus Christ, and to require that her teachings be received and obeyed it can be no other than the Roman Catholic Church; if any has come down in an unbroken line of succession from the apostles, it is this; if any has consistently taught the same doctrines throughout the whole period of her existence, it is this; if any can claim to be the church of the entire Christian world, it is this; if any, by the adoption of all others into herself, would form a consistent, harmonious, and united whole, it is this, and this only. If she has no commission to teach the Gospel, and no assurance that she shall herself be taught by Infinite Wisdom, then no church has, and all which I have said falls to the ground; I am again thrust back into the ocean of doubt and perplexity, with no pilot but my own unaided sagacity, just as I thought I had found a secure harbor.

Now, you start up with the objections always urged by Protestants against the teachings of this church: that they are contrary to the Bible, or that they cannot be found in it; that they are idolatrous and immoral; that many of them are innovations, introduced at various periods since the days of the apostles; that of the ceremonies of the church, some are frivolous and childish, and others are adaptations of heathen rites; that some of the popes have been very wicked men and have sanctioned gross abuses. All these objections I should have urged myself not long ago with the same coufidence with which you urge them now, and some of them are true, as I now acknowledge. Yet my belief that this is the "One Catholic and Apostolic Church" of the Nicene Creed is unshaken by the necessity of making this acknowledgment.

I will take up some of these objections, and give you the replies that seem satisfactory to me. In doing this I expect to say nothing new; nothing that has not been said hundreds of times before; but what I say will probably be new to you, as you have never read anything written by a Catholic in defence of his religion, and are induced to read this, as I suppose, merely by curiosity to learn what the considerations are which have made a Catholic of me.

And first, to the charge that the Catholic Church teaches doctrines which are contrary to the Bible, my only reply is: Prove this to my satisfaction, and I will abandon her at once; the burden of proof rests upon those making the assertion. She herself tells me that the Bible is the word of God, and is to be received and obeyed as such.

But the church teaches things that are not clearly taught in the Bible. This charge, I confess, is well-founded. She teaches, for example, that the first day of the week is for ever to be kept sacred as a day of rest from labor, and of special religious observance; she teaches that the rite of baptism is to be administered to infants, and that baptism by aspersion is valid. You, also, hold these doctrines to be true, and you receive them on her authority alone. If you reject some of her teachings for no other reason than that they cannot be proved from the Bible, consistency requires that you should apply the same rule to all. The plain answer to this objection is, our

Lord sent his disciples to preach, not to write They preached all things whatsoever he had commanded them, and they transmitted to their successors their commission to do so ; but there is no evidence whatever that they wrote, or ever pretended to write, "all things." With the exception of St. Paul, who was not one of the eleven, none of them have written to any extent, and he probably wrote many letters which have not been preserved. Two, certainly, he speaks of himself: one to the Corinthians anterior to that which we call the first, (1 Cor. v. 9,) and one to the church of Laodicea, (Col. iv. 16,) which last he considered of so much importance that he desired the Laodiceans to send it to Colosse after having read it themselves. It is also the opinion of commentators, Protestant as well as Catholic, that the two Epistles to the Thessalonians were written before any others now extant; yet, in closing the second of these, he says, that it may be known as coming from him by the greeting which it contains, written with his own hand, "which is the token in every epistle." These words show plainly that he had been in the habit of writing before this time. Once admit into your mind the possibility that the sacred writings were not designed to take the place of oral instruction in religious truth, but are to be regarded as only subsidiary to it, and the objection, that the church teaches things which are not contained in the written word, disappears at once. She teaches orally what was so taught to her by the apostles, and what has been so taught by successive living preachers from their days to the present.

A more important objection to the Catholic Church is, that many of her doctrines are corrupt innovations, introduced at various times since the early and confessedly pure days of the Christian faith. I have carefully examined the evidences urged in support of this charge—for, if it is true, it is fatal to her claims—and have come to the conclusion, not only that it is not proved, but also that the introduction of such innovations is now, and has always been, impossible. Protestant writers are not agreed as to the precise time when any of these supposed novelties first made their appearance. They assume with regard to some, that they were new in the age in which they are first found alluded to in the writings of the early fathers. But mere silence in regard to any doctrine does not prove that it was unknown. They find detached passages in some of these writings which appear to indicate that the writers did not hold a certain doctrine; but, on the other hand, Catholic controversialists can find quite as many which show that they did. These passages are not, in themselves, conclusive. If the New Testament writers were treated in this way, one man might find evidence enough to prove that they did not believe Jesus Christ to be God; another might collect equally convincing proof that they did not believe him to be man Almost all the truths of Christianity, like the personality of Christ, have a twofold aspect; and it does not follow that a writer who speaks of them under one aspect is therefore ignorant of or rejects the other. If, however, the doctrines now held by the Catholic Church were not held by the Christians of apostolic days, there was a time in the past history of the church when they were first introduced as novelties, and there would be, not such negative evidence as is now adduced, but positive contemporaneous proof of the fact. But Protestant historians have failed to find a syllable of such proof. They cannot produce a word from any of the fathers to show that these novelties were being introduced at the time at which they wrote; not a word of objection to them as innovations; not a word defending them against such a charge.

Take, for example, the doctrine of transubstantiation. The present doctrine of the Protestant churches, the Lutheran excepted, is, that the bread and wine of the Eucharist is nothing but bread and wine from beginning to end, and that the communicant, in taking it into his mouth, takes nothing but bread and wine. The doctrine of the Catholic Church is, that, after consecration, it is, verily and substantively, the body and blood of Christ, and that this body actually comes into communion with the body of the recipient. These two doctrines are as far apart as the north and south poles of creation. A change of faith in regard to this one point is a radical change, altering the whole system, internal and external, of religion. It is claimed by Protestants that the church in the first century held the same opinion in regard to this matter which is now held by themselves. We know that after the lapse of a few centuries the entire church held the other opinion; yet, during the whole interval, no one seems to have been aware that such a change was going on. Is this credible? Protestant writers speak of the change as gradual; but what gradation can there be between these two doctrines? What intermediate resting-place is there between a belief that a piece of bread is nothing but bread, and a belief that it is the veritable body of Christ? I can conceive of none, except an absence of all belief in regard to it.

Equally incredible is it that this change of opinion was gradually adopted, by one religious teacher after another, and one local church after another. We should, then, have one of these two doctrines, so diametrically opposed to each other, maintained by one father of the church, and the other by another; one taught to their people by the clergy in one place, and the other in another, without any controversy having arisen between the supporters of the two doctrines. We know that there has been an uninterrupted succession of Christian writers for and against many of the doctrines of the church; that one heresy after another has arisen, and has been made the subject of abundant contention, until its final condemnation by some general council; that controversies have sprung up which have agitated the whole Christian world in regard to religious questions of far less vital importance than this. Can any sane man believe there was ever a time when the faith of the church was divided between these two opinions, without any contention having arisen to mark such division? Yet Protestant writers do not pretend there ever was such a contention. Some, indeed, refer to the famous controversy of the ninth century, as if it were caused by the first introduction of this novel doctrine of transubstantiation. More candid historians, however, freely admit that the question then in dispute was not whether the sacramental bread and wine became, after consecration, the veritable body and blood of Christ, but had reference simply to the mode in which this change should be explained. The fact itself, as they admit, was believed by the disputants on both sides; the explanation of the fact was fairly open to discussion, as it had not then been defined by the church. It was not the custom of the church to define matters of faith until a controversy regarding them rendered such definition necessary. The doctrine of the Divinity of Christ was never distinctly defined until this was made necessary by the Arian heresy in the fourth century; yet no one pretends to argue from this that it was then a new doctrine.

Again, the fathers of the church have always insisted, as the strong point of their defence in all disputes, that whatever is new is heretical; that their doctrines have been handed down from the apostles, and have always been the faith of the church; and that this is the test by which the true is to be known from the false, constantly quoting the words of St. Paul: "Though we, or an angel from heaven, preach any other gospel unto you than that we have preached unto you, let him be accursed." But such a change as that of which

I am speaking would be the introduction of a new doctrine, not a mere explanation of an old one. The change, as I have before said, goes to the very bottom of the religious system, and modifies more or less every article of the Christian creed. In order to the successful introduction of such an innovation, therefore, it must have been presented to the people as no novelty at all, but as something which had always been taught them; and they must have been induced to receive it, not merely as a truth, but as a truth with which they had always been familiar, and which had been believed and taught them by their fathers before them, though they knew that neither they nor any of their friends or acquaintances had ever heard of it. There must have been, also, a general agreement among all Christian teachers, to begin thus simultaneously to preach a new doctrine as if it were not new; and, while this extraordinary process was going on, of inducing all people throughout the Christian world to believe they had always been taught something which not one of them had ever been taught, not a single sincere Christian arises to protest against such an impious fraud; not a single opponent of the church uses it as an argument against her claims to reverence and obedience.

And remember that all this must have occurred not once only, but over and over again ; for the same argument will apply to the introduction of every one of those doctrines which Protestants call corrupt innovations into the faith of the church, and which no one pretends were introduced at any one time. To me, however, it seems less incredible that there should have been one such change, and only one, to any conceivable extent, than that there should have been a succession of them, each in itself of sufficient magnitude, one would suppose, to stir up a strife that would agitate all Christendom.

This argument, as you will observe, is the same as that which I said, in the first part of my narrative, furnished to my mind the most convincing evidence of the truth of the Christian religion, and to which I then said I should have occasion subsequently to refer. The argument, concisely stated, is this: The doctrines of this religion profess to have been handed down unchanged from the days of the apostles. If they were not so handed down, there must have been some period in past time at which the entire body of the people were induced to receive as old, familiar truths novelties of which no one, until then, had ever heard. This would be impossible *now*, and it has been impossible at *every present time*, however far that time may have now lapsed into the past. If this argument is inconclusive as regards one doctrine, it is equally so as regards any other. If it proves nothing when applied to those held by the Catholic Church and rejected by you, it proves nothing when applied to those held by her and retained by you. If it is possible, or has ever been possible, thus to pass off upon the world a novelty as something always taught and known, we can no longer have any assurance that everything which we now believe as religious truth may not be a purely human invention. The doctrines of the Trinity, of the Incarnation, of the Divinity of Christ, may have had their origin at some time in the first three centuries. The sacraments may have been then introduced for the first time, and men and women persuaded into a belief that they and their parents had been baptized in their infancy, though no one could be found who had any knowledge of such an event; that they had been celebrating "the Lord's Supper," at frequent intervals, all their lives, though no one could remember to have ever heard of such a rite. The sacred books may have been written at the same time, and palmed off upon the people as books which had been read to them all their lives. There may never have been any such persons as Jesus of Nazareth and Paul the Apostle. The narratives of their lives may have been pure fictions, which some ingenious writer invested with such an air of truth, that the whole world, after having once read them, suddenly became totally oblivious to the fact that they were new, and received them as a record of events with which every one had always been familiar.

You will say I am writing nonsense; that such suppositions are ridiculous. So they are. But why? Because you know, and every one knows, that it is impossible to persuade men that they have always been taught what they were never taught; that they have always believed what they never believed; that they have always done what they never did. Yet this impossibility must have become an actual occurrence every time a new doctrine was introduced into the faith of the Christian world; and it must have seemed such a natural, ordinary occurrence that it attracted no notice, that no writer has thought it worthy of being recorded. Compel me to admit, with my present knowledge of past history, that the peculiar doctrines of the Catholic Church are corrupt innovations, never heard of in the days of the apostles, and you compel me to acknowledge that the entire religion of Christians may be a delusion and a fable.

Probably all which I have been saying will fail to produce much effect upon your mind, because, being convinced that the doctrines of the Catholic Church are false in fact and evil in their tendency, you can more easily believe in apparent impossibilities than in the apostolic origin of such doctrines. It is scarcely necessary for me to say that, if your opinions in regard to them are correct, you are perfectly right in rejecting them. I used to regard them just as you now do; but an examination of them satisfied me that, whether they have always been the belief of the church or not, there is nothing in them contrary to the teachings of our Lord and his apostles; nothing the natural and legitimate tendency of which is not to make those who hold them and act upon them pure and holy. I do not intend to take up these doctrines and argue in their defence, as it would require a volume to do this, and such defences are already easily to be obtained by any one willing to read them. But, by showing how you can ascertain for yourself that some of your opinions in regard to the church are erroneous, I may, perhaps, awaken a suspicion in your mind that some other things which you have always taken for granted are equally false.

I used to be told, when a young man, and I have told the same thing to others, never doubting its truth, that Catholics had suppressed the second commandment, because it condemned the worship of images, and, in order to complete the number of ten, had made two of the tenth, transposing the first and second clauses, so as to make an entire commandment of the second clause. Having perfect confidence in the good faith of those who told me this, you may imagine my surprise when I found the missing commandment given entire in all Catholic Catechisms and Prayer-Books, as forming a part of the first. This fact you can ascertain for yourself, without receiving it on my assertion.

As to the supposed transposition of clauses in the tenth, (I am using your method of numbering them,) you are probably not aware that in the fifth chapter of Deuteronomy this very transposition is found, as you may see by referring to it. You will ask, Why did the Latin Church take the commandments from this book, rather than from the original text in Exodus? My reply is, She did not. Her version of the commandments is older than the Latin Bible, older than the Latin Church, or than any Christian church. It comes directly from the Greek Septuagint, which, except in the service of the synagogue, was the version in universal use among the Jews in the time of our Saviour, and from which almost all his quotations, and those of the New Testament writers, were taken. In this Greek translation, the tenth commandment reads in the Book of Exodus just as it does in Deuteronomy. What was the origin of this discrepancy between the Greek and Hebrew texts I have never been able to discover; but certainly the Latin Church is not responsible for it. As regards the method of dividing the commandments into ten, this has always been an unsettled point, and one which has been considered of very little importance; but the division adopted by the Catholic Church is the one found in the "received text" of the Hebrew Bible.

Finally, as to the supposed motive of the church in suppressing the second commandment, open the first Catholic Catechism which you can find, and you may there read, if not in these exact words, in others equivalent to them, the following question and answer: "May we pray to relics and images? We are not allowed to pray to relics or images, for they have no life nor sense, to hear or help us."

I used to believe, and you probably now believe, that it is the doctrine of the Catholic Church, that the absolution pronounced by the priest always confers pardon for past sins, whether the person making the confession is truly penitent or not. Open the Catechism again, and you will find it written thus: "Will a full confession, but without sorrow for sin, obtain our pardon in the Sacrament of Penance? No confession, however full, will obtain pardon for sin, unless we are sorry for having committed it, and resolve to amend." Every Catholic knows perfectly well that the words of absolution are of no use to him whatever, unless he is sincerely penitent, and heartily resolved to sin no more; and he knows that a pretended penitence, which he does not really feel, only adds greatly to the sum of his unforgiven sins. Yet you constantly hear people say, that Catholics cannot be trusted, because they think the priest can wipe out all their sins with a few words of his mouth. I was convinced long ago, years before I thought of ever becoming a Catholic myself, that this is a wretched slander, and that a truly sincere Catholic, who goes regularly to confession and communion, may be trusted with far more confidence than the great mass of even professedly pious Protestants. Those who only call themselves Catholics, without obeying the precepts of the church, are, of course, no better than other irreligious people.

It is often said that the Catholic Church with

holds the Bible from the people. If you wish to ascertain the truth in regard to this matter, you may easily ascertain, that Catholics are directed by their priests to read the Bible ; that Bibles may be found in their houses as well as in those of Protestants ; that they are for sale in all Catholic book-stores, to any one who wishes to buy ; and that the Scriptures had been translated into all the principal languages of Europe, for the use of the people, long before Protestantism was heard of.

It is said that Catholics are guilty of idolatry, of deifying the Virgin Mary, and praying to her as to God. An examination of any Prayer-Book ought to be enough to convince a candid inquirer that this accusation is false. Catholics believe the Blessed Virgin is allowed to intercede for them with her Divine Son, and this is all which they ask of her—that she will pray for them. The most ignorant Catholic knows that the distance between her and God is infinite, and he never confounds the supplications for assistance which he addresses to her, with the worship which he owes to Jesus Christ. If you have any doubt with regard to the truth of this statement, go about among these benighted woman-worshippers and investigate the point for yourself. The strongest language used by standard Catholic writers, when fairly explained, does not go beyond what has just been stated as the Catholic doctrine.

Very many Protestants suppose it to be a doctrine of the church, that the pope can make definitions of doctrine arbitrarily, according to his own private opinions, and that these must be received as infallible. The church teaches no such doctrine. She merely maintains that her divine Founder, in accordance with his promise to be with her to the end of time, so guides all her counsels that everything which she announces as an article of religious faith, or as a doctrine necessarily connected with the faith, is to be received as such. This she must claim, or renounce all authority to teach men what they are to believe. As the faith of the church has always been the same, the only practical use which she can make of her infallibility consists in defining it more exactly, when a controversy arises in regard to the way in which it is to be understood, and in defending it against the heresies to which age after age has given birth, from the days of the apostles to our own times. If the pope himself were to turn Socinian, and declare that Jesus Christ is not "Very God of Very God," it would not change the faith of the church in the least.

You will understand that, in saying no new or corrupt doctrines ever have been or could be introduced into the faith of the Catholic Church, I have had reference only to articles of religious belief defined as such. That many corrupt practices have crept in during past ages, and that many corrupt men have had the exercise of her spiritual authority, no Catholic denies. For centuries before the time of Luther, these corruptions were proclaimed and bewailed by hosts of pious writers and preachers, who exerted all their influence to bring about a reform. But, unhappily, the head of the church, the pope himself, needed to be reformed as much as the inferior clergy; and I am not sure that such a schism as that of the sixteenth century was not necessary, in the providence of God, in order to sweep away these abuses. However this may be, they were swept away; and, since the Council of Trent, the enemies of the church have been obliged, in order to substantiate their charges against her, to go back to the very period when Catholic writers themselves were loudly calling for reform. But it is to be observed that these pious men, while lamenting the wicked lives and corrupt practices of many of the clergy of every grade, never intimate that there is anything that needs reform in the doctrines of the church; not a syllable is uttered by any one to show that he thinks they have been corrupted. This appears to me a fact of wonderful significance. The faith of the Christian world seems, at some periods, to have been entrusted to the keeping of those who feared neither God nor man ; yet they never dared lay their sacrilegious hands upon that faith. Christ himself must have preserved it pure.

I will mention one other objection to the claims of the Catholic Church which has always had more weight in my mind than any other, and which was one of the last to yield its place. It is this : The doctrine of the church is, that her clergy have peculiar authority and peculiar powers conferred upon them by the Sacrament of Holy Orders. They are regarded as the immediate representatives of the Lord himself, and as chosen by him for this office. It seems, therefore, a fair presumption that they would all be holy men. Yet several of them in past times, as is admitted by every one, have been very bad men. How can this notorious fact be reconciled with the doctrine that they were his chosen ministers, through whose hands the gifts of sanctifying grace were to be conferred upon the people ? The presumption against such a supposition would be almost unanswerable, were it not offset by one fact stated in Scripture itself, which shows it to be ill-founded. I refer to the apostleship of Judas Iscariot. It is very likely that you will, at first, fail to see the bearing of his case upon this point, in consequence of your having never thought of him as an apostle, but only as a bad man, tolerated for a time by the rest of the twelve, and admitted among them merely because it was necessary that Jesus should be betrayed by one of his pretended friends. It was thus that I had always regarded him, until it suddenly occurred to me that there is nothing in the gospel narrative to justify such an idea. When our Lord sent out the twelve, he gave them, in proof of their ministry, miraculous powers to heal the sick and cast out devils in his name; these powers were evidently conferred upon Judas just as upon the others. St. Mark says he sent them by two and two, so that there is no possibility of supposing Judas was omitted. Equally impossible is it to suppose there was any apparent difference between his mission and that of the rest, for this would have made him a marked man among them, which he evidently was not. So far was this from being the case, that no one seems to have suspected him even at the last supper, when their Master announced to them that one of their number was about to betray him. He even held a sort of official position among them, having charge of the money which was possessed by them in common. Yet it appears from the words of St. John, that he was a bad man, a hypocrite, and an unbeliever, throughout his whole ministry, though no one knew it except the Lord himself. Here, then, was a man chosen by him—" Have I not chosen you twelve?"—commissioned directly by himself to preach his Gospel, gifted with miraculous powers, in evidence of his mission, and treated by him precisely as he treated those whom he knew to be faithful to him, and yet who never had any love for him, or faith in him as the Messiah, and who finally betrayed him to a cruel death. Now, as everything which our Lord did was designed for the instruction of his disciples in all ages, is it not likely that he meant by this to teach us that, even among his own chosen apostles, we might always expect to find more or less traitors and hypocrites? Does it not afford, at least, a possible explanation of the fact, that there have been wicked priests and bishops and popes, who have, nevertheless, received authority from him to preach his Gospel and dispense his sacraments?

Let us now suppose, for the sake of the argument, that the peculiar doctrines of the Catholic Church are as false as you suppose them to be, how am I the worse for believing them? I hold as true everything which you consider essential to salvation. I believe with you the doctrines of the Trinity, of the Incarnation, of the Divinity of Jesus Christ; I believe that "there is no other name given under heaven, by which we can be saved;" that I can of myself do nothing to merit eternal life; that it is the free gift of God through Jesus Christ, and my daily prayer to him is, "God be merciful to me, a sinner." As I have already said, I presume my former rector would agree with me in all the opinions which I have expressed, except in my being unable to see how the Protestant Episcopal Church of America, or the "American Catholic" Church, as he prefers to call it, is the "One Catholic and Apostolic Church" of his own Creed. You do not think, I suppose, that he and those who hold sentiments corresponding with his, are living in any fatal errors; and if I had retained my connection with his church, you would have felt no apprehension in regard to my future salvation in consequence of my religious opinions. What is there, then, in the doctrines which I now accept as true, that gives you any alarm?

Some persons will say that I worship a piece of bread, and call it my Saviour. If you believe this, you must think me such a fool, that the plea of idiocy should secure me against any future punishment. When I bow down before the sacrifice of the Mass, I am worshipping the Lord Jesus ; whether he is, or is not, present in the consecrated wafer, is a matter of no consequence so far as my intention is concerned, and he will receive my worship just as readily when there is a piece of bread before me, as when there is nothing at all. Even if he be not present in the Host in any peculiar sense, he is so in the same sense in which he is everywhere present. Even on the supposition, therefore, that there is nothing but a piece of bread held up for my worship, what harm does it do me to take just that time to prostrate myself before my crucified Lord?

I bow down and say my prayers before an image of Christ on the cross ; what harm is there in that? I am not praying to the image ; it is merely an external, visible emblem, which serves to bring more vividly before my mind the scene of the real crucifixion. I do not even think of the Saviour as being present in any peculiar manner in the crucifix, but only in the same sense in which you conceive of his presence in your prayers. Protestants treat their bodily senses as spiritual enemies, and shut their eyes when they pray, forgetting that the mind sees even when the eyes are closed. Catholics pray with their eyes wide open, and place some object before them which may aid in the direction of their thoughts, making their senses minister to their devotions.

It is often said that though the use of images and pictures may be unobjectionable in theory, yet practically they lead to idolatry; as the ignorant, forgetting that they are mere memorials, pay divine honors directly to them, and come to regard them as being the realities which they represent. In reply to this I will only say: Go out among the Catholics who abound all around you—many of them are very ignorant—and see how many you can find who think the image or the picture of Christ on the cross is anything more than an image or a picture; how many who believe the image of the Virgin Mary is the Blessed Virgin herself. When you have found one such Catholic, there will be some reason in the objection. While you are doing this, perhaps it would be well enough, at the same time, to see how many bereaved mothers you can find who have gazed at, and caressed, and kissed the picture of their dead darling, until, at length, they have come to regard the picture as the very child which they had lost. You will probably find as many of these as of the others.

I believe that the Blessed Virgin and the angels

of heaven and glorified saints take an interest in the salvation of men upon the earth, and that they are permitted to carry our supplications to the throne of God, and to add their own to ours; and I pray to them to do so. Supposing this to be all a mistake, how am I the worse for believing it? I certainly go directly to God with my prayers none the less because of it, and if any Catholic does, he knows the church forbids it. If the angels and saints do not hear my prayers, the worst that can be said about them is, that they are useless. The idea that there is anything wrong in asking a dead friend to pray for us, even on an erroneous supposition that he can know and comply with our request, seems to me absurd. Protestants quote the text: "There is but one mediator between God and man, the man Christ Jesus." Yet they have no hesitation in asking others to pray for them, and in praying themselves for others. Praying for another, therefore, is not assuming to act as mediator between him and God; asking the prayers of another is not asking him to act in any such capacity for us. Indeed, the very chapter from which the above text is taken begins with an exhortation that "Prayers, intercessions, and giving of thanks be made for all men." Now, if it is right and proper in me to ask you to pray for me, it makes no difference where you may be, or how the request may be sent, provided it can in any way be made to reach you. If you were in England, I might despatch it by telegraph, and you would think it perfectly proper. If you were on the planet Jupiter and I could send it to you there, you would see no harm in it. If you were in heaven, and I could send it to you there, why might I not? You say, you would not receive it. Very well, then it is lost, and that is all the harm that has been done. I certainly am none the worse for having tried to send it; and if, as you will probably admit, no one ever asks another to pray for him, without, at the same time, resolving to pray for himself, I shall have derived some benefit from the attempt, even though it has been unsuccessful.

But it is not true that a belief in this doctrine is useless, even if it be erroneous. There is a natural longing in the human heart to bring earth into closer communion with heaven than the almost infinite distance at which Protestant theology separates them. If you could yourself believe it to be true that glorified saints and blessed angels are ever watching over you to guard you against sin, and are praying to God for you night and day, you know that such a belief would so encourage you in your resolves to resist temptation, would so strengthen you in every holy purpose, that your life afterward would be very different from what it was before. You wish, you cannot avoid wishing, that this doctrine were true. If you could be convinced of its truth, you would clasp it to your heart and thank God for it. But did not God know that his weak, erring creatures upon earth would long for this intimate communion with heaven? Did he not know that they would derive incalculable benefit from it? Was he not able to grant it? Why, then, should we doubt that he has done so? And if, as I have said, men are made holier by a mere belief in the doctrine, is it credible that so strange an effect could be produced by their believing a lie? Is it possible that, by wandering from the path of God's truth, I become more careful to obey his commands than I was before thus straying into error? Let those believe this who can; I cannot.

I believe in the existence of purgatory. Suppose there is no such place; what harm results to me from a belief in it? What is this doctrine of purgatory? It is, that very few persons, however holy their lives may have been in this world, are fitted at the moment of death to go immediately into the presence of God, to join the glorified company of heaven. That it is necessary for them to pass a longer or shorter period in an intermediate state of existence, in which, through the suffering of temporal punishments, they may be freed from all the consequences of the sins which have been pardoned by the grace of God. Am I less likely to strive after holiness, believing this doctrine, than if I thought that, no matter how wicked my life may have been, I should go from my death-bed directly to the realms of eternal blessedness, provided only that I repent and resolve to amend when it is too late to put my resolution into practice?

I ask again, therefore, supposing the peculiar doctrines of the Catholic Church are not true, what harm shall I suffer from a belief in them?

You will say, perhaps, that it must, in the very nature of things, be injurious to any one to believe what is false and to act upon that belief. Admitting that this is so, it is shifting altogether the question under discussion, and in order to decide whether it is you or I who will be injured by the faith we severally hold, it must first be settled which of us is believing what is false. You claim that the Bible must decide. So do I. You claim that each must study the Bible for himself, and judge for himself what it teaches. So do I. So far we are agreed. But I find it taught in the

Bible that our Lord instituted a church which should remain through all ages as the authorized expounder of his truth, which church I am bound to acknowledge and obey. This you profess yourself unable to find. We differ, therefore, as to the teachings of the Bible, and who shall decide which of us believes what is false, and therefore injurious to his soul? Where is the umpire to pronounce judgment between us? If we can come to no other agreement, we must agree to differ, until God, in his infinite wisdom and goodness, shall mercifully interpose, and show our errors to whichever of us is in the wrong; and that for Jesus Christ our blessed Saviour's sake he will graciously please so to do, should be your prayer and mine, day and night.

And now, do not suppose that, in consequence of having become a Catholic, I no longer regard you as a Christian, or that I intend to exalt myself above you in holiness or sincerity of purpose to do the will of God, or that I accuse you of wilful sin in having never examined into the claims of the Catholic Church to your obedience. I know perfectly well that you have never had any more idea that it was your duty to do so than that you ought to read the Koran of Mohammed or the New Gospel of Joseph Smith. Until a little more than a year ago, I have always had precisely the same opinion myself, and my conscience does not reproach me for not having done what I never suspected it was my duty to do. God, in his mercy, as I verily believe, opened my eyes to see that some things were false which I had been taught with regard to the Catholic faith. Having thus aroused my interest in the matter, he has led me on, step by step, to my present entire confidence in a church which I had always believed to be utterly corrupt, and wholly given over to work abominations. If I, with my present opinions, were to reject the claims of this church, or neglect to join her communion, through fear of alienating my friends or injuring my worldly prospects, or from a repugnance to the class of worshippers who throng her temples, or from a want of sympathy with them in some of the collateral services which may seem to you better adapted to the tastes of children than of grown men; if for these, or any other reasons, I were to refuse her sacraments, I should be guilty of mortal sin. But the church makes every possible allowance for those who, like you, believe and trust in Jesus Christ, and sincerely desire to know and to do the will of God, and who are kept from her fold only by an ignorance so absolute and intense that nothing but the almighty power of God can dispel it. She pities you and prays for you, and commends you to the mercy of our loving Lord, but she pronounces no curses upon you.

At length, my long task is ended. I have been in no haste in writing these pages, but have taken time enough to be sure of my convictions before declaring them to others. Four and a half months have passed since I began this writing, and during this period my mind has been almost constantly employed upon the questions which I have been discussing, and every day has added to the assurance which I feel, that I have come to a right decision. I hope that, having read what I have written, you will admit that there is, at least, some show of sense in it. If you think my reasoning false or my conclusions erroneous, show me where the error is, and if I see it, I will cheerfully acknowledge and renounce it; for I solemnly declare and appeal to him who sees my inmost heart as the witness to what I say, that I believe my only desire is to do the will of God and my Saviour Jesus Christ, and to secure the salvation of my own soul. The moment I find I have made a mistake in joining the Catholic Church, no false shame or dread of inconsistency will prevent my abandoning it.

Does it not seem to you a singular thing, that so

many men, of late years, who have begun to examine the claims and doctrines of this church, with an honest admission that they may possibly be well-founded and true, and with a sincere desire only to ascertain the truth, have ended by entering her fold, while, so far as I know, not one such person has decided against her? How do you account for this very extraordinary fact? I believe you have always given me credit for an average share of intelligence and good sense; but some of these men are giants in intellect and learning in comparison with me. Yet, according to your ideas, they have been induced to adopt as truth falsehoods so apparent to every person of ordinary intelligence that they deserve only to be laughed at. If error in regard to matters of eternal interest can so assume the appearance of truth as to deceive such men, who can be sure that any of his opinions are correct?

Again, does it not seem a singular thing, that no sooner does a Protestant begin to manifest an interest in the claims of the Catholic Church, than his friends become alarmed, and some by entreaties, and others by ridicule, endeavor to persuade him to banish the subject from his mind? Is this a reasonable or intelligent way of treating a question of so much importance? If the claims of the church are so palpably false as you suppose, cannot you credit your friends with enough common sense to enable them to see the fact for themselves?

Yet once again: does it not seem to you a singular thing that in every public controversy between Protestant and Catholic theologians, it has been admitted by uninterested spectators that the Catholic champion had the best of the argument? Yet if you will take the trouble to inquire into this matter, I think you will find it to be true. The famous Hughes and Breckenridge controversy occurred when I was at Princeton, and I well remember that the decision of all those students, whom I heard express an opinion in regard to it, was, that Mr. Breckenridge was fairly beaten. If he succeeded in answering the bishop's arguments, why were Protestant papers so careful not to let their readers know what those arguments were? And why has no Protestant publisher ever given the public both sides of the controversy? It appears to me that, after having demolished an enemy's fortress, vanity, if nothing else, would induce the victorious general to show the world how strong it was.

It is very possible that you will close the perusal of these pages with no other feelings than those with which you began it—wonder at my perversion from the faith of my parents, mingled, perhaps, with a little contempt of my folly. If so, I shall have written to very little purpose. For my object has been, not merely to justify in your eyes the step which I have taken, but also to arouse in your mind a suspicion that there must be something worthy of examination in arguments that have proved convincing to me. If you should be conscious of any such suspicion, I beseech you not to shut it out as foolish. I began with such suspicions myself, and they led me to examinations which strengthened them, and I have now no doubt that it was the voice of the Blessed Spirit which was whispering into my ear. He may be doing the same thing with you; be careful, therefore, how you turn away and refuse to listen. Your eternal welfare may be put in jeopardy by so doing.

My prayer for you, and for all whom I love, is, that God will make known his truth to you. You can certainly have no objection to this prayer, nor to making the same for yourself. I hope you will also unite with me in praying that we may all, brothers and sisters, parents and children, be united in the one fold of Christ here below, worshipping and serving him together upon earth, acknowledging one Lord, one faith, one baptism, and be gathered together hereafter in heaven, to worship, and praise, and enjoy him for ever. May God grant this, in his infinite mercy, for Jesus Christ's sake!

www.ingramcontent.com/pod-product-compliance
Lightning Source LLC
LaVergne TN
LVHW021358110826
845150LV00007B/1698

* 9 7 8 1 4 2 5 5 1 3 2 2 1 *